God's Colony
in Man's World

God's Colony
in Man's World

George W. Webber

Abingdon Press

NEW YORK • NASHVILLE

GOD'S COLONY IN MAN'S WORLD

Copyright © 1960 by Abingdon Press

Library of Congress Catalog Card Number: 60-9203

E

SET UP, PRINTED, AND BOUND BY THE
PARTHENON PRESS, AT NASHVILLE,
TENNESSEE, UNITED STATES OF AMERICA

To

all God's beloved in East Harlem, who are called to be
saints and who seek to follow Jesus, who read in the
synagogue:

> *"The Spirit of the Lord is upon me,*
> *because he has anointed me to preach*
> *good news to the poor.*
> *He has sent me to proclaim release to*
> *the captives*
> *and recovering of sight to the blind,*
> *to set at liberty those who are oppressed,*
> *to proclaim the acceptable year of the*
> *Lord."* (Luke 4:18-19.)

Contents

Contents

God's Colony
in Man's World

INTRODUCTION

In the spring of 1948 four Protestant denominations agreed to begin an experimental, store-front ministry in the East Harlem section of New York City. Executives responsible for city mission work were by and large sincerely troubled about the failure of Protestantism to remain in our inner city areas and looking for any kind of new pattern that might be tried. The East Harlem Protestant Parish became a symbol of the new concern with Protestant witness in the city. Within a short time eight denominations were united in this Protestant ministry. Substantial resources of money and personnel were made available, not only from home mission budgets, but from individuals and church groups all over the country. Freedom was granted the staff to try a variety of approaches and experiments in the one central effort to confront the people of East Harlem with the good news that Jesus is both Lord and Christ.

In the early days of the Parish the staff was besieged with requests for speaking engagements. People wanted to learn about the problems in such a community and about the work of missions there. Most of the speeches were designed to tell the story of the Parish, to trouble the conscience of the listeners about the needs of the inner city, and to elicit support for substantial missionary work of this and similar types. But in recent years the tenor of the requests for speeches has sharply changed. Again and again the staff is asked to use East Harlem and the experiences here as a mirror that might reflect, for the more typical Protestant churches, something of the life and mission of the church. The substance of this book was called forth by the invitation of the Montview Presbyterian Church in Denver to give a series of five lectures, using the experience in East Harlem to reflect on the task which challenged this large congregation far removed by every kind of obvious human difference from the people of East Harlem. The underlying assumption was that the gospel does not change from one community to another, nor is the fundamental nature and task of the church determined by sociological, cultural, or any other kind of human factors. We who are engaged in the ministry in East Harlem witness here to the lordship of our common king and seek to discover the patterns of our life as Christians which are relevant to the day in which we live.

These chapters are an effort by one group of Christians to share with their brothers, for the sake of our common edification, how the battle is going on in our sector of the frontier. In so far as the experiences of East Harlem are used, it is only in the hope that they point to our common task and may assist in understanding the nature of mission wherever God has placed his witnesses. Such understanding is desperately needed by American Protestantism, often too busy to ask what its own busyness is all about. In East Harlem the challenge and frustrations of the inner city forced this question to the fore. The staff began in typical American fashion. They saw the acute human needs of the community. They knew, in faith, that in the gospel was the answer to human need. It was their task to bring together the needs of the community and the power of the gospel. God did not allow any simple equation. The staff was driven to rethink the meaning of the gospel, the nature of the church, and the doctrine of the ministry. These are urgent, even desperate, matters.

14

In the process great insight came from men and women who, in our own day, are living in missionary situations. We have tried to digest in American terms the theological perspective and wisdom which have come to us from men like Hendrik Kraemer, George MacLeod, D. T. Niles, Ernest Southcott, Bishop Newbigin, Ted Wickham, and others.* These European friends have already faced the fact that the church is always in a missionary situation and have been thinking ahead of us about the nature of the church's mission. Through their eyes we have come to understand more clearly what we are about in East Harlem and in the process have had to realign much of the program and work we have undertaken.

The chapters which follow are neither the story of the East Harlem Protestant Parish nor an analysis of its theological position. The experience of the Parish is drawn upon only in the hope that it might illuminate the task of every Protestant church that is seeking to understand its mission. But in order to begin on common ground, it is necessary here to sketch briefly the East Harlem background out of which the author writes.

The community of East Harlem is clearly defined by geography. At 97th Street the New York Central Railroad tracks emerge from under Park Avenue and run on a trestle to the 125th Street Station. Where the trains emerge from the tunnel, the wealth of Park Avenue, in one block, gives way to the slums of East Harlem. On the west the boundary is Central Park and Fifth Avenue, and on the east, the river. Here in a little over one square mile live approximately 215,-000 people. Some sociologist estimated that if everyone in the United States lived in the same density as these 215,000, the entire population of the country could be contained in half the geographical boundaries of New York City.

To most people the name Harlem suggests the Negro ghetto that

* See Bibliography.

lies north of Central Park. In reality East Harlem is a world of its own, with a long history as an immigrant community. The tenement buildings at East Harlem were built to house the great mass of immigrants that poured into the United States around the end of the nineteenth century. One after another the immigrant waves have swept across the community, leaving a deposit of those who did not readily move into the main stream of American life, or who preferred to continue in the familiar community in which they first found their way into America. The community at present has a substantial Italian population, though this is rapidly decreasing as the major population groups become migrants rather than immigrants. The Puerto Ricans have come in a steady stream from their tropical island, especially since the close of the Second World War, and Negro families move to New York from the South. Both Negro and Puerto Rican families face a serious problem in adapting to the culture of New York City. Added to the problems of the earlier immigrant groups is the problem of color, which makes it much more difficult for them to be assimilated into the melting pot and move out of East Harlem into the Bronx and eventually into one of the suburbs.

There has always been a rootlessness about the people who live in this neighborhood. East Harlem has been a place where the immigrant gained a toe hold in America. As soon as he made the grade, he moved out. The same psychology holds today. Everyone who moves into the community, whether it be into a tenement or into one of the great new public housing projects, expects shortly to move. As a matter of fact many of the Negro and Puerto Rican families will be there for the rest of their lives. But as long as they are dominated by the psychology that this is a temporary situation, there is little reason to become involved in the organizations which give a real heart and character to a neighborhood.

At present East Harlem is more than ever a community of great human need. Here the whole range of social problems, created by modern urban life, is seen in exaggeration: race prejudice, juvenile delinquency, inferior schools, poor housing, breakdown in family life, loss of meaning in work, and all the rest. Here one sees in stark terms the meaning of depersonalization, the fearful trend in our society to make human beings into objects to be manipulated, exploited, or organized.

In East Harlem the challenge to the church is inescapable. With all its great and obvious need East Harlem, like numerous similar communities, has baffled Protestant efforts to maintain a vital Christian witness in the inner city. The Protestant Settlement House made a genuinely selfless attempt to serve the newer immigrants where attempts at Protestantism were all but hopeless. But as tides of immigration brought Jewish and Catholic families into the community, many churches closed. A few managed to maintain enough of their former Protestant membership to keep the doors open. By the close of the Second World War the assumption was generally held that Protestantism had little reason to be in these inner city communities.

A rather superficial test indicated how false this assumption was. On a lovely spring Sunday in 1948 two seminary students planted themselves at either end of a crowded East Harlem block at 6:00 in the morning. For seven hours they kept track of people who left the block, on the assumption that they might be going to church. More likely they would be off to visit relatives in the Bronx. In that seven-hour period only thirty people left the street who might conceivably have been going to church. On this block were living at the time about two thousand people, almost equally divided between Negro and Puerto Rican. Puerto Rican families are supposed to be Roman Catholic, and the Negro families are the strongest Protestant group in New York City. The fact that only thirty, at the most, attended church on a warm Sunday in Lent was good indication of the utterly godless nature of that block, certainly typical of the whole East Harlem community. It was estimated that at best only 20 per cent of the people in the entire community ever set foot in a church or synagogue during the course of the year.

Here, where there was such an obvious concentration of human need, the church was notably absent. In 1948 there was not a single Protestant church of a major denomination ministering with any effectiveness to the people who lived in East Harlem. There were only a few Protestant churches left, and these were characterized more by their iron gates, locked except on Wednesday night and Sunday morning, when a few former residents returned for services, than by their ministry to the community.

The combination of the human need of the community, the un-churched character of its population, and the absence of any effective Protestant witness set the stage for the unique, interdenominational co-operation that led to the East Harlem Protestant Parish. Together the denominations could find the resources for a major project. The initial plans were accepted by the mission executives of four denominations: American Baptists, Congregational Christian, Methodist, and and Presbyterian Church, USA. They were soon joined by the Reformed Church in America, General Conference Mennonites, Evangelical and Reformed, and Evangelical United Brethren.

In a remarkable degree the East Harlem Parish was given freedom to experiment with all kinds of techniques and programs. Often the Parish has been irresponsible and sometimes has transgressed the line between the foolishness of God and just plain foolishness. But only in trying a wide variety of approaches would vital patterns for communicating the gospel emerge. The field of liturgy, for example, was one in which the whole history of Christian worship suggested ideas for experimentation. Rather than subject all the churches of the

Parish to this experimentation, one clergyman, with a particularly vivid imagination, was asked to work out creative forms of worship with his local congregation. When, out of the many things tried, something seemed to be valuable and useful, it would then be incorporated into the worship of the whole Parish.

The ministry of the Parish has been directed toward one area, the lower eastern quadrant of East Harlem, roughly from 96th to 112th Streets, between Lexington Avenue and the East River. Within these boundaries over 25,000 people live, both in the old deteriorated tenements and in the newer high-rising public housing projects. The Parish employs the following facilities: three store front churches, begun in the early days of our ministry; a Presbyterian church, formerly a mission to the Italian community; two rented club rooms, used for work with two street clubs; two apartments on One Hundredth Street to serve as a base for a fine medical clinic; a store front headquarters for work with drug addicts; a large office in a former furniture store on Second Avenue, where there is also a Federal Credit Union, legal aid clinic, and library; and a retreat center, fifty miles from the city, used extensively for week-end retreats and in the summer for family camping.

From the very beginning the work of the Parish has been characterized by several basic assumptions. First was the idea of the store-front church. If the gospel were to be communicated to the people of East Harlem, it must be presented on their level, in a framework which would be natural and direct. We discovered that in East Harlem the normal pattern of community organization on the crowded tenement blocks was the store, laundry, or social club. Here were found the natural social grouping of the gang, of young adults, of mothers, and the rest. The sect religious groups used rented stores as their base of operation. Should we not develop the same pattern? Within a few months of the beginning of our ministry several store fronts were rented on crowded tenement blocks. In the middle of 100th Street, for example, with its four thousand people, a small store was found that rented for fifty dollars a month. It was about twenty by twenty-five feet, with sagging floor and rotting ceiling. Here was a base of operation from which to begin a ministry to the people who lived on that block. With its plate glass window, making the interior clearly visible, and a door on the street level it was a place into which people could come easily, as they walked down the street with their needs and problems. During the week the store front could be a meeting room, a recreation center, and office for the minister. On Sunday it was transformed into a sanctuary with folding chairs, a communion table in the center, and a pulpit with an open Bible. Through the use of store fronts, with their modest rent and minimal amount for maintenance, most of the funds of the Parish could be invested in personnel. This stands in contrast with the typical inner city situation in which a large and often deteriorated building demands as much for maintenance and heat as can be paid in salary to the minister. It also provides a mobility and freedom to move in the face of a changing neighborhood.

The second assumption, which has become something of a symbol of the East Harlem Protestant Parish, was the need for a group ministry. Instinctively, those responsible for the first years of the Parish began as a team. The group ministry meant a multiple approach, using people with supplementary skills and abilities. It meant a sense of comradeship and mutual support in the face of discouragement and frustration. It also included the wives of the staff, giving them the possibility of participation in the ministry of the whole Parish in a unique way. In a very real sense the early development of the Parish, as a genuine unity of the newly formed churches, was made possible by the unity within the group ministry. The fact that the staff was bound together by a common set of disciplines and by a common budget had a distinctly unifying effect. The disciplines of the group have undergone certain changes over the years but have basically been designed to establish the minimal patterns of life which are necessary for the Christian in his obedience to Jesus Christ. Although at first designed for the clergy, the general necessity for a discipline of life was thought to be imperative for the whole membership of the Parish.

The third basic assumption has to do with social action. The Parish has always stood for the relevance of the gospel to human need. The church that acknowledges Jesus Christ as lord must offer his love to those who stand in any kind of need. At the same time the church must join Christ in his battle against evil in the world. Its members must fight for justice, and in whatever ways are open, seek to overcome the problems that distort life in East Harlem.

The continuing ministry of the Parish is in no sense an indication of any discovery of successful answers to the task of communicating the gospel in the inner city. In the course of over ten years the Parish is only beginning to feel at home in East Harlem, and through its participation in the common life of the community, gaining the right to speak directly of the meaning of the gospel. But it is just possible that here the church is face to face with the crucial issues which must confront Protestantism in our day. Part of the frustration of much that the church does in our time may come from the fact that it is engaged in the wrong fight, giving its energy to battles that are finally irrelevant. We hope that in East Harlem the issues confronting the church, the struggle to discover again the nature of the Christian community and the mission of the church are at least on the right frontiers, and that as we wrestle with these questions, we are dealing with issues which are of significance wherever the church seeks to be faithful to its Lord. If the churches of America do not struggle with these same issues, the gospel stands in danger, not so much from the world as from the church itself.

CHAPTER I

THE NEED FOR NEW WINESKINS

> And no one puts a piece of unshrunk cloth on an old
> garment, for the patch tears away from the garment, and a
> worse tear is made. Neither is new wine put into old wine-
> skins; if it is, the skins burst, and the wine is spilled, and the
> skins are destroyed; but new wine is put into fresh wineskins,
> and so both are preserved.
>
> Matt. 9:16-17

This book is born out of the ministry of the East Harlem Protestant
Parish, in the crowded upper East Side of New York City, but it is
not the story of the church in East Harlem. It is a consideration of the
nature and task of the church in our day, forced upon us by the frustration of twelve years of struggle against the apathy and sometimes
antagonism of a modern urban community. The traditional forms of
the churches we knew as children and young men in middle class
America have little power or relevance in a community like East
Harlem. No matter whether it was a question of organizing Sunday
schools and using the traditional curriculum, or the style of preaching
on Sunday morning, or an evangelistic program along the lines of
visitation evangelism, it hardly seemed to matter. Tried and true ways
of communicating the gospel often were of little use.

In this kind of frustration we have been driven to seek again to
understand the nature of the church itself. Perhaps this is rationalizing
in the face of the limited success or even failure of Protestantism in
the inner city. More hopefully, it is a valid and imperative function

of our very nature as Protestants. From our heritage we are aware that the forms and institutions which men create in response to the gospel quickly take on their own patterns of sinfulness, which make them less than full instruments by which the mission of the church may be fulfilled. Every age, perhaps in our time every decade, demands a new Protestant Reformation. The wineskins into which, in each new day, the gospel must be poured have to be continually renewed, or they are burst open and become useless. It would appear beyond question that in the modern urban situation new wineskins are definitely needed if the gospel is to be contained and thus made available to a desperately needy world. Through no virtue of its own but out of the very situation in which it found itself enmeshed, the church in East Harlem has been driven back to the need to find patterns for its life which are appropriate to the day in which we live. Although in the chapters that follow there will be some rather explicit suggestions about possible new patterns for our day, it is the need to search for such patterns as fully as success in finding them, which is the pressing need for every church in every day.

A. The Foolishness of the Gospel

The gospel is the same yesterday, today, and forever. It is the same in suburbia and in the inner city. It is this basic presupposition which justifies the assumption that the task of the church is one wherever the gospel is proclaimed. There is an inescapable link between every church, which means that we in the inner city may expect to learn about our task from our brethren in the more successful Protestant church and vice versa. It also justifies the suspicion that the seeming success of the churches of suburbia and the striking failure of the churches in the inner city both reflect a desperate need for genuine renewal. The failure of the gospel to gain a hearing in the inner city and the too easy acceptance of its message by the churches in suburbia both point to the failure of the church to take seriously the radical nature of the gospel.

A key text for our time is the first chapter of Paul's first letter to the Corinthians in which he speaks in strenuous terms about the scandal of preaching and the foolishness of the gospel. Is he right in declaring that to men who seek to live by their own wisdom the gospel is always foolishness? A gospel which centers on a cross and finds victory in death makes no sense whatsoever, either to suburbia or to East Harlem. A gospel which turns life upside down and demands that we make every human loyalty subsidiary to our allegiance to Jesus Christ flies dead in the face of everything that men naturally find acceptable. When men too readily accept the gospel, when our churches are accepted as a good thing for the American way of life, are these not warning signals that the forms by which we are carrying on our Christian life have lost the power to contain the gospel? The once strong wineskins by which American Protestantism expressed its life have grown old and obsolete without our noticing that at many points they have sprung subtle leaks or even split wide open. Again and again our European Christian friends who visit this country are amazed at the vigor and energy which they see in the immense activities of our churches. But when they dare to be honest with us, they can almost always be counted on to ask sharp questions about our certainty that the energy thus invested is being used in the task to which God calls us, that of witnessing to the Lordship of Jesus Christ over the church and the world. "How," I have been asked, "have the American churches gotten around the folly of the gospel and the foolishness of God and somehow made the gospel so palatable to people that your churches are successful and prosperous?"

I do not think such questions can be shrugged off as European "sour grapes." Must not these questions trouble every one of us if we permit ourselves to ask serious questions about the radical nature of Christian obedience? Recently, an able and dedicated group of clergy, drawn largely from suburban churches, gathered for a discussion of evangelism. The one issue uppermost in all of their minds was the problem of converting those who had already become members of their churches. To these ministers this was a really serious and baffling concern. Something was wrong when they admitted people into membership in the body of Christ, permitted them to take the sobering vows of obedience, when in fact the lordship of Christ had little or no meaning in their lives. These clergy were in agreement that drastic steps were necessary. As one of them quoted, "The time has come for judgment to begin with the household of God" (I Pet. 4:17).

In every time of reformation men seek to go back to the New Testament. This is the basis for our knowledge of the event by which God's salvation is made known. It is also the story of the new community, the church, through which God chose to make known the gospel to all men. In the New Testament we see the new community, the colony of heaven, set in the midst of a hostile and antagonistic world as a witness to the kingdom of God which has broken into history. The need for us in America to immerse ourselves in Scripture is too obvious to argue. Only as we are steeped again in the Old and New Testaments does the gospel take root in our lives. By the same token it seems more and more logical to look with fresh eyes at the pattern of life in the New Testament church. In East Harlem we have discovered that there are far more parallels between the life of the little struggling churches in the New Testament world and our own situation than we had ever imagined. Perhaps we have not dared to take seriously the witness of these young churches because the quality of their obedience and of their foolishness was beyond that which we are willing to affirm.

B. The Modern Urban Situation

In our modern world of rapid change it is not surprising that our human institutions have fallen behind the pace of modern life. Our churches are still functioning with nineteenth century patterns in the middle of the twentieth century. The assumptions we make about life no longer have much relationship to the facts of our time. Sunday school literature which assumes that children live in houses, come downstairs for breakfast, and play out in the yard is mostly out of date for millions of youngsters growing up in the cliff dwellings of our modern cities. The Protestant emphasis upon individual responsibility makes little sense to men caught up, in almost every area of their life, in a matrix of forces completely beyond their control. Methods of evangelism, once powerful instruments in confronting men with their predicament and claiming them for Jesus Christ, now fall on deaf ears. In a word the Protestant churches, which have placed tremendous emphasis upon individual responsibility and the concern for individual men and women, now find themselves in the midst of a depersonalized world which has made obsolete many of the patterns we have long taken for granted.

The key word is "depersonalization," a condition of modern society described with considerable force by social psychologists, sociologists, as well as an increasing number of theologians. One reads books like *The Organization Man* and *White Collar* to discover that depersonalization describes vividly the whole tenor of relationships in modern industrial life. Not only the families of East Harlem but middle income college graduates now live in vast housing projects where their name is one over a thousand doorbells in a great concentration of human beings. A college friend accepts a management position in a paternalistic firm which takes seriously its responsibility for the whole life of its employees. His wife is told which flower circle of the hospital guild she belongs to, in relationship to his status in the factory, and he is told that he is to teach in the junior-high department of the local Presbyterian Church, since this is "expected of executives in his position." This is not the unconscious depersonalization of a great factory in which men are treated as units in production or as cogs in a machine. This is conscious depersonalization by which human beings are manipulated through all the techniques of modern psychology. It may be that the fundamental expression of sin in our day is to make the other person into an object and thing.

The church in the inner city sees in utter starkness the relationships of depersonalization. There it is quite possible to discover a twelve-year-old child for whose life every relationship with the world is one in which he is treated much like an object rather than a human being. His life is denied love from anyone in the family matrix; he finds himself in a junior high school for which he is inadequately prepared and unable to make any academic progress, harassed by the police, whom he looks upon as an enemy, forced into a gang for some kind of protection and status, given medical care by the utterly impersonal clinic of a vast city hospital, and even when his life is touched by professional social work, he is apt to be treated as a case rather than as a living human being. Depersonalization is finding seventeen people living in four unlighted, unheated, and unventilated coalbins beneath a building on One Hundredth Street in East Harlem. Depersonalization is sitting for five hours waiting for treatment in the emergency ward of a public hospital. Depersonalization is living in a public housing project in an apartment to which the management has access without your permission any hour of the day or night.

In East Harlem one sees with incredible starkness the depersonalization of our modern world. If, however, depersonalization does in fact characterize our whole society, then East Harlem is not a backwater of modern America, a place where certain problems have not yet been solved, but rather a place in which one sees more obviously than elsewhere the basic problems with which our society is confronted. When one lists the crucial problems which face the people in East Harlem, they sound very much like a similar catalog in the *Atlantic Monthly* or the Sunday magazine section of the *New York Times*—racial discrimination, inadequate housing, broken homes, overcrowded schools, juvenile delinquency, alienation from meaning in work, problems in the use of leisure time. Paul Tillich suggests that in modern art and literature one sees in sharp delineation the brokenness in modern life. Perhaps our East Harlem presents something of the same ominous portent. If this assertion is true, then the task which the church faces in East Harlem has a very direct relevance for the task of the church anywhere in American life.

C. The Predicament of the Churches

A true church is an outpost of the kingdom of God, placed in a particular spot in the world to bear witness to the Lordship of Jesus Christ. A church is a mission living by the foolishness of God in a world that sometimes hates it, sometimes is indifferent, and sometimes seeks to take it captive. Any church that does not recognize the basic purpose for its existence is in jeopardy of its life. The predicament of the church in America is precisely that it does not recognize that it is in a missionary situation. Missions are seen only as a special project of the church, through which men and women are sent overseas to preach in distant lands. Even the local mission of the church is a home missionary venture off somewhere in Indian territory or in the world of the inner city. We have forgotten that mission is the task of the church wherever it finds itself. There are many ways in which this basic predicament can be illustrated.

1. THE DISUNITY OF PROTESTANTISM

The multiplicity of denominations in America is good indication of our failure to take, with sufficient soberness, the missionary character of the church. When a church truly recognizes that its gospel stands against the values of the world and when it is true to itself, it is always being challenged by the world. Then of necessity its members are driven to stand together and seek to discover anew the unity which in fact has been given them by their common allegiance to Jesus Christ. The relatively easy acceptance of our denominational differences in America points to our failure to recognize the seriousness of the task which confronts us.

Perhaps we are all too accustomed to seeking out our own kind rather than truly evangelizing. This is to say that our heritage, as national churches or as denominations with a message to a particular group, has taught us when we seek to find new members to look in our community for those who are of our own cultural or religious background. We cull out our own kind and in the process fail to confront vast segments of society with the claims of the gospel.

Wherever in our world the mission of the church is again being taken with seriousness, almost inevitably there are real pressures toward reunion. In countries where Christians are confronted with rival religions, the drive toward reunion is very apparent and obviously necessary. I suspect the time will shortly come when the growing movement toward reunion in the United States will take on an urgency that it does not presently have. There have been significant church unions in recent years but not always motivated by a desire more faithfully to fulfill the mission to which God calls them.

Not only is the mission of the church plagued by denominational divisions but also by the divisions within our churches along class lines. Few indeed are the congregations which represent a broad cross section, even of their own community. By and large our churches are defined along cultural or class lines. George MacLeod of the Iona Community likes to tell about a little city in Scotland where there were five churches, all located in precisely the right places in terms of their cultural characteristics. The Baptist Church was near the river; the Salvation Army was by the fire house; the Methodist Church was next to the gas station; the Episcopal Church was by the drapery store; and the Presbyterian Church was halfway between the ice house and the bank. These class divisions are often justified as a logical corollary to our natural human differences. People argue that we must come together along the lines of our human unity and that a given congregation will naturally be filled with like-minded people of a somewhat similar cultural background. The fact that the early church was able to bring together, into the little household fellowships of the church, the slave and the wealthy master, the educated and the uneducated, must be a judgment upon us. Here people of incredible cultural differences were able to live together in a unity that somehow broke through the differences of class, culture, and education. That this is possible may seem unbelievable, but it points to the mystery and power of the gospel.

The church is also plagued with divisions along racial lines. The Protestant church has been made well aware of its failure to witness to the gospel which unites people across racial divisions. Continually reminded of the segregated character of our congregations and the slowness of our progress in this field, we still do not face the concrete implications demanded by the gospel.

I recently was asked to speak on the topic of race relations at a lovely suburban church. My hostess was quite pleased that I had been able to come and speak on such a timely topic, even though she did not feel that for many in the room the issue was a very pressing concern. As she said, in the community in which the church was located

31

no Jew or Negro was permitted to buy a home, so the congregation did not really face the problem of race relations in any intimate way. Was it wrong to suggest to that group that the gospel demanded that they, as a congregation, stand against the evil of discrimination in housing and seek to open their community to Negroes? I doubt that there is any congregation in this country, however remote, that does not have within the bounds of its community a sobering problem of racial discrimination and about which the church has probably been silent, if not ignorant.

But the minority groups are aware of our failures at this point. The first time I ever went calling in East Harlem, I had been assigned to a tenement building with thirty-three apartment units. I started at the top floor, but before knocking on the first door, I saw the janitor, who was mopping the floor. I introduced myself with all the enthusiasm of a young clergyman and was met with the response, "I am glad to meet you, Rev. Webber, but we might as well understand each other right now. I ain't got no use for the church, and I ain't got no use for preachers." The scorn in his voice was obvious. His bitterness, it turned out, came from his feeling of real rejection by the Christian church on the grounds of his race. He knew more than I about the bitter treatment which the Negro people had received at the hands of Protestant churches. We must confess that our divisions along racial lines, no matter how unavoidable they may seem, are devastating to our witness to the unity in Christ, in which there is neither bond nor free, Jew nor Greek.

2. THE IRRELEVANCE OF THE CHURCH TO SOCIAL ISSUES

A church historian recently said that at no time in the history of America have the Protestant churches been so successful in reaching a large percentage of the population, but also that at no time in our history had the church been so irrelevant to the social issues of our day. In a word the Christian must have a concern for bad housing, segregation, the causes of juvenile delinquency, the threat of atomic destruction, and all the rest. But we have no word of the Lord with which to confront our society or any real thought that in the gospel there might be perspective or direction in facing these issues. Religion too often has to do only with our personal life, the religious compartment, with nothing to say to the issues in the arena where our daily life is lived. For most of us religion has become one of the twenty-five departments in *Time Magazine;* it is an area, an interest in our life, but not the focus through which the problems of our existence are understood and our direction determined. We have nothing to say to the world, and the world knows it. Often the church is silent. Often when we do have some word to speak, we are afraid to say it. Often when we do speak, the words we say are irrelevant, "ideal mongering" that is not directed to the centers of power in our society but an idealistic demand for justice or brotherhood that sounds good but is in no way in contact with the dynamics through which change comes.

This irrelevance of the church is, above all else, a denial of the incarnation. Jesus Christ came into the world that the world might be saved. Through the power of his life, death, and resurrection the world is different. Jesus Christ is Lord. The church must live in history as witness to his Lordship. We in fact know the truth about the world, and we must speak this truth with power and directness. It is the truth about the world which the world needs to know. If we are to take Jesus Christ seriously, then we must live by the incarnation in and for the world.

3. THE CHALLENGE OF FALSE GODS

Men must worship. It is given in our nature that we must seek for some object of our ultimate loyalty and devotion. We are not able

33

to live without identifying our life with some purpose or meaning. From the point of view of our biblical faith the alternatives are clear. One may give his allegiance to the God, who is our Creator, Sustainer, and Redeemer, in Jesus Christ, or one must find some false loyalties, some little gods, by which the meaning of our life can be established. In our day it is clear that many gods clamor for the allegiance of men, and often we are worshipers of a whole pantheon, finding value or meaning now in one direction and now in another. In a community like East Harlem the alternatives are quite obvious.

There is the religion of escape. In part incidence of narcotics addiction can be explained by the need of adolescents to find some kind of way out of the frustrations and meaninglessness of their lives. Alcoholism, another age-old form of escape, is a prevalent religion of East Harlem. The religion of rebellion was symbolized by the strength of the communist element in East Harlem in 1948, but also by the incidence of lawlessness and gang warfare. But perhaps the main religion of East Harlem is simply that of apathy. The effect of depersonalization is to grant people an empty freedom which cuts them off from all commitment toward their fellow men and toward society. The day by day crises of existence make it difficult to live with any sense of perspective or hope.

One of the most tragic illustrations of this apathy that I have come across is in a study of truancy in a local junior high school. A group of sociologists, studying the school population, discovered a group of about twenty boys who were chronically truant. They investigated their background to see what was involved in their lack of interest in school. To their great surprise they found that the boys were not, as they had supposed, playing hooky in order to play baseball, get in some kind of trouble, go to the circus, or what have you. Rather, they discovered that the twenty boys were to be found almost any time of the day or night sitting around the house. Perhaps they were not out of bed or were staring out the window or listening to the radio. When queried as to their hopes or plans for the future, the boys indicated quite clearly that they had no hopes, no plans, no dreams for the future. Can you imagine the real distortion of human life when there is no future to it; "where there is no vision, the people perish." In a very real sense depersonalization had taken its final toll. When the past has no experiences of meaning or significance for our lives, and when there seems to be no future that offers any hope or meaning, when the future is crushed in on the present, then we really exist on an almost animal level. Vision and transcendence have been taken away. In a very real sense these boys were the victims of total depersonalization. They lived a life of sheer apathy. If the gospel is to speak with power in this kind of world, it must literally bring people from death to life.

Not only is there the challenge in East Harlem of false religions, there are also the challenges from the sectarian and sometimes heretical groups. The presence of Jehovah's Witnesses through the community X is tremendously apparent. They call with relentless regularity through the public housing projects and make not a few converts by the intensity of their faith and the confidence and authority with which they speak. The Jehovah's Witnesses are a problem to people who are basically courteous and hospitable. In discussing the attacks of the Jehovah's Witnesses with some of our own parishioners, we have always encouraged them to admit the Jehovah's Witness if he would promise to grant them equal time. The only trouble is that most Protestants are utterly unable to make use of such time with any kind of confidence or effectiveness.

On every block in East Harlem there are almost sure to be several store-front churches, running all the way from small fundamentalist Baptist congregations to the most exotic and esoteric sects. In the Puerto Rican community in particular there are many Pentecostal churches, whose appeal has been very strong. In the course of preparing the groundwork for the East Harlem Protestant Parish several of the ministers visited a large number of these store-front churches and found always a genuine welcome from the worshippers. Often the pattern of worship had elements of great integrity and power which might well be introduced again into our traditional Protestant churches. These sect groups remind us often of the pattern of life within the early church. There is an expectancy in the minds of the worshippers, a degree of fellowship and concern, which is truly of God. At the same time one cannot escape the judgment that by and large the store front churches of the community provide an escapist religion focused upon the life to come and in no way taking seriously the fact that God made a world that was good, and we are to live in the world even though our final hope lies outside the world. You cannot blame people who live in misery and poverty for finding their meaning in this kind of escape. It is clearly a judgment upon our society and upon the Protestant church that this alternative comes with both power and necessity.

In summary one recognizes once more the missionary character of the neighborhood. The vast number of citizens in the community have no relationship to any of the traditional religious bodies or to the store front churches. It is false ideologies and attachments to various human groups which are necessary in order to justify their existence. Here the light of the gospel seems nearly extinguished by the powers of darkness and evil. In a time of so-called revival of religion the failure of Protestantism in the inner city points to a tragic failure at the very center of our culture. Here at the point of greatest human need and most human problems we are at our weakest. The religious situation in the inner city is clearly a missionary challenge in which less than 20 per cent of the residents maintain an active affiliation in any church. American Negro families, traditionally strongly Protestant, and Puerto Ricans, supposedly Roman Catholic, seemed neither to maintain their religious heritage nor to develop any new religious affiliation amid the pressures of urban life.

Is it not obvious that the false gods of suburbia are not too different in quality from the false religions which offer some kind of meaning to the people of the inner city? The tremendous American interest in religion, as so many writers have pointed out, has become a very general and vacuous business, more concerned about supporting "a way of life in the American style" than in obedience to Jesus Christ.[1]

4. FALSE PATTERNS IN OUR CHURCH LIFE

Another symbol of the predicament of the churches and their failure to understand the nature of their mission in our present world is suggested by the patterns of evangelism which have become part of our church life. In a city like New York Billy Graham may indeed lead a tremendous religious revival which calls those of Protestant allegiance to a renewal of their faith. But it seems impossible to consider his mission primarily evangelistic. Such a crusade is not necessarily evil; it is simply irrelevant. In the depersonalized world of the city a preacher, no matter how powerful, speaking in Madison Square Garden, makes virtually no impact upon the great mass of people who have not been nurtured in the Christian faith. They have long since stopped listening to the ranting of ministers of whatever stripe, whose peculiar jargon fills the airways and the TV screens. It may even be that the day of the great pulpit minister is passing. Few younger clergy these days seem able or willing to pay the price of real pulpit mastery in the style of former days. The demands of their varied ministry make it impossible to give the necessary time and energy to this aspect, which in the past has demanded such a tremendous block of a clergyman's time. In part this is unhealthy, for the preaching of the Word must be recaptured as a central aspect of the church.

[1] See Will Herberg, *Protestant, Catholic and Jew.*

The point here is another one, that men and women in our day are less and less influenced by the power of the spoken word unless it is the beginning of a genuine dialogue or conversation carried on in such a way that a response is demanded. The spectator attitude, which is being driven deeply into our lives, has robbed the preaching of the Word of some of its power, for men are not accustomed to responding in depth as they sit before a TV screen or listen to a speech.

Again, one wonders about the usefulness of visitation evangelism when the literature seems to assume that this great emphasis in many of our denominations is designed primarily to locate the people in the community who, by their background and culture, are logically part of a fellowship of our church. It may legitimately fit under the heading of evangelism, but too often this method nets only men and women who have already been within the orbit of the Christian faith. One doubts its effectiveness in confronting the pagans who are emerging in our midst in modern life. In a word it does not presuppose a radical missionary situation but is rather a form of recruitment for our churches.

In these and many other ways one suspects that our churches, with all their vitality and energy, are not devoting themselves to the crucial tasks which God has set before them. The gospel judges us and, in the judging, makes renewal possible.

D. *The Gift of the Gospel*

The predicament of Protestantism, so ominously seen in the inner city, does not spell defeat for the church. God does not reject his people. He is seeking to call us back to faithful obedience. But renewal will come as God's gift when we honestly face our situation and, with repentance, acknowledge our failures. Even this ability to see honestly into our predicament is not something we can decide to do but comes as a gift of God. In the inner city, through no virtue of their own, God has granted that Christians see the dimensions of our human problem. There the old wineskins have burst or deteriorated in such obvious ways that no one can overlook the seriousness of the situation before the church. The whole range of modern urban problems, as well as the inadequacy of the church, have reached such an advanced stage that their true nature is clearly revealed.

When men and women see their human situation honestly, recognize the need for love in their lives, God may lead them into the way of salvation. In this light we see the grim problems of the city not as problems which we must solve but as God's way of leading us back to dependence upon him as the Lord of Life. In the gospel, not in all our human efforts to change society or ourselves, is the hope of us all. When God casts us into the heart of modern urban America, confronts us with the predicament of the church, he is in fact offering us the gift of new life in Christ.

In the context of our repentance God offers us also the gift of new wineskins. When a church honestly sees its dependence upon God and accepts with sorrow its failures, it may hope that it will recover "that open, dynamic life into which the Holy Spirit pours His gifts." [2] God has prepared for us the channel through which to serve him. But we must discover what these new channels are. In the inner city the search cannot be avoided.

The patterns that are not of God simply do not work. So often in our day men join the church or think they accept the gospel without having really been confronted with the radical claims of Jesus Christ. Or they reject the gospel without having really glimpsed it. In the inner city the possibilities of such deception are much less. The confrontation is usually sharp and honest, for the church is not "a good thing" nor the gospel an accepted part of a "way of life." The world looks with suspicion upon the gospel and is not easily forced to face the question:

[2] Visser 't Hooft, *The Renewal of the Church*.

"Choose ye this day whom ye will serve." The search for new forms is the effort to find God's ways for our time with which to confront men with Jesus Christ in such a manner that a genuine decision is forced upon them—either to accept him or reject him. Thus the test of new forms is their power to contain the gospel, to witness to and demonstate to a suspicious, hostile, or apathetic world that Jesus Christ is both Lord and Savior. Such forms will have to do with the pattern of life of the Christian community, with the work and witness of Christians in the world, and with the ways in which we speak to our brother about Jesus Christ. In all these areas the church that seeks to serve its Lord in the city is continually searching for the patterns that will serve the gospel. Such searching is the necessity of every Christian community. But it comes as a gift of God.

Hidden amid this situation of the city where God grants his people the gift of insight into their predicament and leads them to seek new wineskins of obedience is the greatest gift of all. Here God raises up people who reveal in their own lives the possibility of a life of faith in the midst of despair and tragedy. He gives us evidence of his power to transform and redeem human life, no matter how hopeless the situation seems, by giving us the gift of men and women whose lives have been filled with love. As a young clergyman, called to East Harlem to proclaim the gospel, I have in fact been ministered unto by the saints whom God has called forth in the midst of what seem to be overwhelming human problems. A mother, struggling to raise a large family on a welfare budget, with no husband in the picture, is yet able to accept God's love as real, to turn to him in time of trouble, and praise him for the joy of living. Burdened down with deep human troubles, seemingly up against impossible odds, she does not fight false battles for status or material values but accepts her dependence upon God's grace and lives by trust in him. And this is not an escapist faith. The love of Christ within her overflows to her neighbor in need, in service to her church, and concern for her community. Through her God speaks to me, for her faith mirrors for me the shabbiness of my own life. Through her the gift of the gospel takes on a new reality. Now one who seems so different in cultural terms has become my brother in Christ, and our oneness in him takes on new meaning. Together we seek the new patterns for our common situation in order that we may serve our Lord and in East Harlem witness to the power of the gospel that has restored us both to life.

41

CHAPTER II

THE PURPOSE OF THE CHURCH

Holy Father, keep them in thy name which thou hast given me, that they may be one, even as we are one. . . .

But now I am coming to thee; and these things I speak in the world, that they may have my joy fulfilled in themselves. I have given them thy word; and the world has hated them because they are not of the world, even as I am not of the world. I do not pray that thou shouldst take them out of the world, but that thou shouldst keep them from the evil one. They are not of the world, even as I am not of the world. Sanctify them in the truth; thy word is truth. As thou didst send me into the world, so I have sent them into the world. And for their sake I consecrate myself, that they also may be consecrated in truth.

John 17:11, 13-19

One of the best ways to avoid living by the gospel is to spend time discussing the doctrine of the church. A whole shelf of books has been written on this subject in recent years. In theological schools it is the center of a great deal of debate and concern. Christians are called by God to be and to act, not endlessly to discuss. Yet it is impossible to continue further without putting down certain definitions which will help make clear what it is the church must be and do. There is, of course, the added danger that in defining the purpose of the church one will so idealize what it is that the church must be that no possible expression of this doctrine will ever be a reality in the life of men.

The church is the means which God chooses for saving the world. This is its purpose. The church is the result of the mighty acts of God in the life and death and resurrection of Jesus Christ, by which something decisive for the whole of history took place. Presumably, God could have chosen other means; we simply confess that it is through the church that the event is to be proclaimed to men, both by the life and work of the church. Jesus did not leave behind primarily a code of ethics or a set of principles for life, but a group of men who were bound together by their knowledge that he was their Lord and Savior. "As thou didst send me into the world, so I have sent them into the world." (John 17:18.)

T. R. Morton, deputy leader of the Iona Community in Scotland, argues cogently in his little volume *The Twelve Together* that Jesus in fact refused for several years to open the eyes of the disciples to what his ministry was all about. They had to share a new way of life before they could comprehend it. He called them into a community with him, dependent upon God's grace for their daily life, united by a unique style of fellowship unlike any they had ever known, and sent by their commitment to God and life together on a mission in the world. It was this life together that was the news of the gospel, this fact of reconciliation between men, their oneness in Christ, that in reality the brokenness, alienation, and separation of men from God has been overcome. In life together the power of sin is broken.

For this reason the New Testament customarily uses human analogies, rather than institutional ones, in speaking of the church. The basic figure by which the church is described is "the body of Christ." It is quite clear that when Paul speaks of the body of Christ, he is not using a metaphorical phrase; for him, in a very concrete way, the church was the extension of the incarnation. Now, in the present tense, Christ is alive in the world through the church, his body. It was the body of which Christ was the head, and it lived by the power of his grace. Again and again Paul seems to look directly at a congregation and say to them, "You are the body of Christ, you as a congregation gathered here together." And then looking at each of the individual members he reminds them, "And you are individually members of this body." To live by the reality of this truth is to turn the lives of men and women upside down.

It is exciting to see the results of looking upon the church primarily as person and not as institution. Then when we speak about the work and activities of the church, we no longer use institutional verbs like "promote," "administer," "indoctrinate," and "succeed." Rather we find ourselves using such words as "serve," "teach," "preach," and "suffer." Whenever the church gathers together as a congregation, it celebrates again the events of the gospel. Its worship is in fact an event itself, for God makes new his promises and his presence each time believers gather to offer him their praise and thanksgiving. God here and now is renewing his people; here and now a new word breaks forth by the power of the Holy Spirit, through God's presence in preaching and worship, the Sacraments of Baptism and the Lord's Supper. Then God sends his people forth to do his work in the world, to live by the gospel, to offer men the love of Jesus Christ, and to witness to his lordship over the world. The church in history continues the ministry of Jesus Christ.

A biblical metaphor from the Moffatt Translation serves to define further the content of the definition of the church as the body of Christ. Paul addresses the Philippians thus: "You are a colony of heaven" (Phil. 3:20). This phrase, better than any other I know, catches up the essential missionary character of the life of the body and helps define the new wineskins for today. The churches of our time, whatever their situation, need desperately to recognize that they are outposts of the kingdom of God, called to witness to the foolishness of the gospel in a world that threatens their very life.

Any metaphor can express only part of the truth, and has within it

44

certain dangers. The word "colony" clearly can imply imperialism in a very unfortunate sense. Let me suggest, however, certain real values, which I think this particular figure of speech has for our situation, by suggesting the parallel with the early pilgrims as colonists on the New England coast. In such a colony three basic facts of their existence were "existentially" apparent. First, the colony was utterly dependent upon the homeland if it were to be sustained in the middle of a hostile world. Only the infrequent ships bringing supplies and new personnel along with encouragement from the homeland made it possible for the colony's life to be continued. It was the lifeline to the homeland which could not be severed if the colony were to continue in strength during those early years. In the second place there was an unmistakable unity which surrounded the lives of the colonists. They were all in the same boat. If a child contracted smallpox, the lives of everyone were in danger. If the Indians attacked, all had to come to the defense of the colony. They were, in a unique sense, made into one family. Finally, the colony recognized that its only reason for existence was its work in the world. Although by night it was necessary to withdraw behind the stockade for protection from the Indians and the marauding beasts, the work of the colony was outside the fence, in the tasks of subduing the wilderness and bringing it under the lordship of the colony's own king. The work of the colony was in farming the land, fishing the streams, and colonizing the Indians. The colony in its own interior life existed only to make possible the task of the colony in its dispersed life in the world.

These three dimensions can be applied clearly to the purpose of the church in our time. The vertical dimension reminds us of the absolute dependence of the congregation upon the sustaining grace of God. A church which does not meet primarily in worship to acknowledge God's gift of salvation and to seek there renewal of purpose and devotion is not a church at all. A church which, in its own life, acts as

though it were a democracy in which the rule of the majority was decisive rather than a theocracy in which the rule of God must be decisive is not a true church. We in the clergy so easily lapse into the
natural way of speaking about "our church," which again, in a very
subtle way, can betray our forgetfulness that it is only Christ's church
of which we dare speak. Or the vestry, session, or other governing body
of the church can so easily forget that even in the most mundane
business decisions about the administration of the life of the church
there is a point of reference which stands over the secular wisdom of
men, and only at their peril can it be forgotten or ignored. When the
church comes together, it is to celebrate the gospel; it is to remember
and re-enact the event in which the reconciliation between God and
men was accomplished in Jesus Christ. It is the church's celebration of
the presence of God with his people. God is in the midst of the congregation when his people gather to hear the word preached and the
word made visible in the sacrament. Our celebration is both memory
and hope and present reality, in all of which we acknowledge with
thanksgiving the power and grace of God.

The circular dimension of the colony is another significant way of
speaking about the church in our time, if one may use the expression
"circular dimension." This refers to the quality of our life together, of
the unity which is the characteristic of those who know that Jesus
Christ is Lord. Mark that the vertical dimension is always first. Human
beings are made one as brothers only because Christ is their Lord.
There is much too much sentimental talk about the brotherhood of
man. This has no reality, for me at least, and I think not for the Christian church, apart from the prior acknowledgment that Jesus Christ
is our point of unity. It is only when we confess him as Lord that we
are driven by the implications of this fact to recognize in my brother
one for whom Christ died and thus one to whom my life is inescap-
ably tied. Whenever the church does recognize the fact that it is in a

46

missionary situation, it is instinctively drawn together in solidarity, drawn together for reasons not dissimilar to the solidarity of men on a ship in wartime, faced with the common threats to their lives.

Perhaps the horizontal dimension is the one about which the church must have its greatest concern in our day. The church exists for its mission in the world. This is obviously true in East Harlem, but it is as necessarily true of the church in any situation. Between the foolishness of the gospel and the values of suburbia there is a battle which the church must wage. In the face of all the petty idolatries of men the church must witness to the reality of the one true God. In the face of all the desperate efforts of men to find some kind of community, which fulfills our natural human need for fellowship, the church must witness to the reality of the God-given community which comes through Jesus Christ. This is not simply to stand on the street corner and talk about Jesus Christ—or more likely preach on radio or TV— to a world that has long since stopped listening to talk about the gospel. I keep remembering a passage in the book by George MacLeod, *Only One Way Left:*

When I was in South Africa, just prior to a big public meeting in Durban, an unknown ulsterman approached me and said, "I hope you are going to give them the Gospel red hot." "Yes," I replied, "I am speaking of its social implications here in Durban." "Social implications?" he repeated in an acme of suspicion, "what is wanted is the Gospel red hot." "But is it not of the Gospel," I asked, "that by the right of Christ all men have an equal dignity?" "Yes," he said. "That is of the Gospel." "Then what," I said, "are you Gospellers doing about the 10,000 Africans and Indians who have not got a decent shelter in Durban this cold night?" "Them?" replied the hot Gospeller, "I wish the whole damn lot were sunk in the harbour!" Yet that man could have recited the whole Christian offer immaculately, and his own engagement to be in Christ.[1]

[1] *Only One Way Left* (Glasgow, Scotland: The Iona Community House, 1956), p. 54.

In another place he writes,

I simply argue that the Cross be raised again at the centre of the market place as well as on the steeple of the church. I am recovering the claim that Jesus was not crucified in a Cathedral between two candles, but on a Cross between two thieves; on the town garbage heap; on a crossroads so cosmopolitan that they had to write his title in Hebrew and Latin and in Greek (or shall we say in English, in Bantu, and in Afrikaans); at the kind of place where cynics talk smut, and thieves curse, and soldiers gamble. Because that is where he died and that is what He died about. And that is where churchmen should be and what churchmen should be about.[2]

But the market place is a battleground in which we must contend "against the principalities, against the powers, against the world rulers of this present darkness, against the spiritual hosts of wickedness in the heavenly places" (Eph. 6:12). The colonist lives dangerously. In East Harlem the antagonism, suspicion, and apathy of the world toward the church is very apparent. Between the Church's proclamation of the gospel and the world there exists a clear gulf. The battle lines are marked off sharply and the conflict strong. Precisely, the reverse is true for many other Protestant churches in America. Instead of a clearly outlined frontier along which the sharp foolishness of the gospel is apparent, the world seems in fact to have engulfed the Church. The values of the world have become the values by which the Church lives. The Church has become something acceptable and natural. The Church is "a good thing."

Several years ago a seminary student was called for the summer to a little church in a small town in Arizona that was able only to have a pastor during the summer months. He said it was wonderful to arrive in town and find that he was welcomed by everyone. The men

[2] *Ibid.*, p. 38.

were so pleased that the women would have a church to attend. The mothers thought it was fine for their children. Young people thought the church would be a real help for the old people, and the old thought it would help solve the problems of the young. The only trouble, the young minister said, was that he could find no one in town who thought that his coming had any particular significance for him. The churches of America, too often captive to the values of our secular world, need desperately once again to recognize that between the values and truth of the gospel and the values and truth by which the world lives there is a frontier. A faithful church is always in a colonial situation.

Our work as colonists is made possible only because the territory assigned to us has already been claimed by our Lord. The colony seeks to call the world back to its rightful ruler. The Bible speaks in very concrete terms about the way in which in Christ the principalities and powers of evil at war with God in the world have been defeated. "He disarmed the principalities and powers and made a public example of them, triumphing over them in him." (Col. 2:15.) Christ, who is Lord of the Church, is also Lord of the world. We do not go from church into the world as a place from which his power is absent. Rather we go into the world, where Jesus Christ is Lord, in order that the news of his kingship might be proclaimed, "that through the church the manifold wisdom of God might now be made known to the principalities and powers in the heavenly places" (Eph. 3:10). It is for the sake of serving him, who is the Lord of the world as well as its own Lord, that the colony lives.

At the same time the world is still a dangerous place. The principalities and powers of evil, which for Paul were as concrete as the Roman legions and Caesar, are still very real. The enemy does not, in fact, know that its defeat has been accomplished. This is the secret and hidden wisdom which had been made known to those who confessed their faith in Jesus Christ. Thus, the colony which lives for the sake of

49

the world must yet protect itself in the world. The world is a place where there is still great danger from all the forces of evil which oppose the king. Our life, in a very real sense, is one of rhythm from the battle of life in the world back into the sanctuary of the church, where vision may be renewed by the preaching of the Word, our bodies fed by the sacrament and our courage renewed in the community of our fellow soldiers. What we do within the life of the church are not pious exercises but rather preparations directed toward our mission in the world. It is our sins in the world which we confess to God when we gather in the church. It is the concerns of our life in the world for which we intercede. It is the ordinary bread of daily life which we break in the sanctuary as a reminder that whenever we break bread, we should give thanks to him who sustains us in all of life; and when we are in the world, we are sustained there by the knowledge that at the end of our labors there is a place to which we may return. For the Christian in the fullest sense the work of his life is an offering to the Lord of the church. He works in the world but is sustained by his life in the colony. He is undefeated in the world because his true home is not of the world.

CHAPTER III

THE LIFE OF THE CHURCH

Now there are varieties of gifts, but the same Spirit; and there are varieties of service, but the same Lord; and there are varieties of working, but it is the same God who inspires them all in every one. To each is given the manifestation of the Spirit for the common good. To one is given through the Spirit the utterance of wisdom, and to another the utterance of knowledge according to the same Spirit, to another faith by the same Spirit, to another gifts of healing by the one Spirit, to another the working of miracles, to another prophecy, to another the ability to distinguish between spirits, to another various kinds of tongues, to another the interpretation of tongues. All these are inspired by one and the same Spirit, who apportions to each one individually as he wills. For just as the body is one and has many members, and all the members of the body, though many, are one body, so it is with Christ. For by one Spirit we were all baptized into one body—Jews or Greeks, slaves or free—and all were made to drink of one Spirit. . . . Now you are the body of Christ and individually members of it.

I Cor. 12:4-13, 27

The Christian community, a body of those called from darkness into light by the power of God's grace, exists to *worship* and to *witness*. The whole life of the church must revolve around these foci. To give glory to God by its corporate worship and sacramental life and to serve his purpose by its existence as a colony in the world—these define the

51

whole meaning of the church's life. The wineskins which are appropriate for the life of a colony must be judged by their capacity to contain these twin tasks of worship and witness.

In this chapter we are concerned with this quality of life which rightly characterizes a church and how the structures and forms, the new wineskins which we devise, can assist the purposes of God in bringing into being such a community of worship and witness.

A. A Description of Koinonia

It is significant that when the New Testament speaks about the church, it is not referring to a building on a corner but always to a fellowship of Christians, whether in a regional or a city or local sense. The church is people meeting for worship in someone's home. The church is a council of those gathered together to consider their faith. The quality of life of this church is defined by the word we translate "fellowship" and in the Greek *koinonia*. Fellowship, like so many of the great biblical words, has been so much used and misunderstood by the world that it bears little resemblance to its biblical meaning. Every church would claim to be a fellowship, but it may be using this term quite clearly in the fraternity house sense of fellowship. There is a universal human need for community that in our day finds expression in an incredible proliferation of ersatz communities. Men need desperately to live together, but in all human communities we find means of exclusiveness or ways in which we may clearly limit the amount of our involvement.

The fellowship of the church is a different matter. *Koinonia* implies a fellowship of men and women, of all sorts and conditions, who are united by one fact, that Jesus Christ is their common Lord. It is our vertical relationship with Christ which makes possible and inescapable our horizontal relationship with every fellow Christian. When men truly accept Jesus Christ as Lord, then and only then are they made one family. There is no place for exclusiveness among those who have made this simple, and yet transforming, confession of faith in Christ. The colony is thus a genuinely open fellowship, open to men of every station and color, yet closed to any man who does not accept Jesus Christ as Lord.

There is no place for limits upon the amount of time we allot to our involvement in the colony. This startling fact sets the church apart from every human community. We cannot allocate a section of our time and interest a certain number of evenings each week. To accept Jesus Christ as Lord and enter into his company is to accept a new vocation, a full-time position with a lifetime contract. We are now marked with his sign and witness to him in every moment of our lives. It is a truly radical word to accept the fact that Christ lives in us, that we are his body, that by every action of thought, word, and deed we are witnessing to our Lord, however broken or distorted this witness may be. When we accept the mark of Christ, the world inevitably will judge Christ by us.

Part of the trouble in our definition is that rarely have any of us experienced any genuine confrontation with *koinonia*. We occasionally glimpse it or have some small feeling of it, but too often we have used the word carelessly in applying it to experiences that hardly deserve the term. The young people's conference, gathered around the fire on a lovely mountain side, experiences a tremendous sense of fellowship, but this is more than likely an experience of human togetherness that has little of the depth of our unity in Christ.

When ministers talk, as I am writing here, about *koinonia,* we have every right to be challenged by the world. "Show us what you're talking about. I don't get all the theological words that come pouring out. Where can I go that I can taste and feel what *koinonia* is all about?" Even in the midst of New York City, with its many great churches, this request would be somewhat baffling. Where would one want to take the unconvinced person in order that he might feel the power of the Christian community in depth and reality? Perhaps you would respond that it isn't so simple as all this; you can't expect someone to come into a church and in one or two visits find the depth of true community that exists. I'm not so sure, however, that in the house churches of the first century the pagan was not confronted with a startling awareness that something here was different. Was it not precisely the power of the early church that men and women, living in the Roman world, saw that in the church wealthy women, slaves, and soldiers came together in Christian love and oneness? This was so shattering a miracle that the world had to take it seriously. As was said then, "Look at those Christians; see how they love one another." The world is always astonished when disunity is overcome by oneness. This is the miracle of the Christian fellowship.

If I wished to provide an analogy for *koinonia* to someone who did not understand what I was talking about, I would be tempted to expose him to one of the sect groups, where far more of the powerful spirit of the early church seems to pervade than in our great middle-class organizations. Before the East Harlem Protestant Parish began, several of the ministers visited nearly one hundred store-front churches throughout East Harlem. Again and again they found themselves caught up in the power and meaning of services whose patterns were utterly foreign to them. The participation of the whole congregation in worship, the way in which deep human concerns were brought into the life of the congregation through the prayers spoken by individuals, the welcome which they received as strangers—all of these pointed to something of the essence of *koinonia*.

A quite secular analogy to *koinonia* is felt in a meeting of Alcoholics Anonymous. AA is open to anyone who is an alcoholic and knows in fact that he is powerless by his own efforts to defeat his problem. Only when he recognizes his utter bondage to his problem and is willing to rely absolutely on the power of God and the support of his brothers can he really be part of the organization. Even when he has been able, through the organization, to maintain his sobriety for a long period of time, the alcoholic never forgets that he is still in bondage to this problem. It is still a very real threat, in spite of his present triumph. A testimony at an AA meeting always begins, "I am an alcoholic," even though you discover that he hasn't had a drink in fifteen or twenty years. Alcoholism remains his continuing problem. The alcoholic lives one day at a time, praying only that he may have the strength to live that one day without a drink. He is always available day or night to assist a brother alcoholic. Here the crucial element of unity lies in common human bondage, whereas for the Christian unity comes from the common Lordship of Christ. But the analogy to *koinonia* is impressive.

In terms of biblical faith Christians are a company of "sinners anonymous." The Christian knows that the ultimate problem of his life is his own sinfulness, and he does not become a Christian until he discovers that he cannot lick this problem on his own, that he needs the forgiveness of God made known in Christ and the support of his brothers. As long as he lives, sin remains his problem. It is this fact which insures the openness of the church to the world. We have not achieved some special status in terms of our moral purity which puts us in a paternalistic relationship to our fellow men. The Christian is still a sinner who recognizes his solidarity with every sinner and whose heart is filled by compassion for those who do not know the forgiveness which is freely offered in Jesus Christ.

This, however, is right at the heart of the foolishness of the gospel. There are few of us brought up in America who relish the idea that we are dependent upon God, or far worse, dependent upon our brothers. Doesn't it honestly make us somewhat uncomfortable when we are confronted with these words? We are taught to stand on our own two feet, to bear our own burdens, and particularly, to mind our own business. We do not want somebody supporting us, nor do we want to have to support anyone else, unless, of course, *we* want to. We are afraid to trust our fellow men; we are afraid of what they might do to us and what they might demand of us.

We do, in fact, live in a broken world. It is the power of the true colony that it points to the restored community. It is a witness to the truth that in Christ men have been brought again into unity one with another, in which we dare to be honest with one another, in which we are not afraid because we are willing to admit the truth about ourselves.

In spite of the obvious failure of many churches to approximate the kind of fellowship known in the New Testament, the fact remains that in the midst of every congregation there are aspects of unity which are very real. The critical impulse often drives us to overlook what God is doing, or worse, to demand of God that he grant us a degree of *koinonia* that we have already determined is our right. If we would accept gratefully whatever unity has been given to us and pray with repentance about our own disruptiveness in the household of faith, perhaps God will bring forth even greater unity. You cannot create *koinonia*. The fellowship of the church is a gift of God. God gives one the grace to love another person; one cannot, by gritting his teeth, determine to do so.

B. Structures of Our Common Life

At the same time there are structures of our common life which make possible our openness to the Holy Spirit and the kind of relationships with our fellow men in which *koinonia* may indeed become possible. The reverse is also true. The present structure of activities in most of our churches seems to me to make necessary a fellowship along lines of our cultural homogeneity and almost impossible the creation of genuine unity in Jesus Christ. When the women's club spends its afternoons sewing, the talk will almost certainly be along lines which demand a certain natural human community from those present. When the basic time of men within the church is spent on business matters, there is little chance for our oneness in Christ to emerge.

At great danger of oversimplification or suggesting a method for getting at something which cannot be gotten at by any method, I would offer a direction in which I think the life of our ordinary congregation must move. The clue comes from the Protestant Reformation. It was the genius of the Reformation to look back to the New Testament and seek again to find new wineskins for its message. The Reformation said to men and women who had never been able to hear the word of God preached in a language which they could understand or read it in familiar words, "Now the word of God is something you may hear and read." For the first time sermons were preached in the language of the people; the Bible was read in a tongue that was familiar, and equally important, they were able, for the first time, to taste the living word in the Sacrament of bread and wine. This new reality, the preaching of the word, and the participation in the sacramental life of the church was so exciting and so overwhelming that it set men running. A whole new movement and direction took place in the life of the church.

I am persuaded that the stress on Word and Sacrament is an emphasis which we must recapture in our day. It is bedrock on which we must build, if God's word is to be lived with the exciting, transforming, and renewing power that was experienced in the sixteenth century. But the reformaton emphasis for our day is not a return to Word and Sacrament. These make the necessary base for what is new, but the reforming word for the new wineskins in our day is *koinonia*. It is the common life of the church which must be the beacon on the hill to all the world. When the world sees Christians gathering in love and unity, it will have to stop and look.

1. THE NEW FOCUS: THE ENABLING GROUP

Concretely, this means that the center of the life of the church must not simply be the worship on Sunday morning, where the Word is preached and the Word is received. This Reformation emphasis must be supplemented by an equally strong emphasis on our participation within the life of the church at points where the problems of our obedience in the world will be considered. We must participate in the common worship life of the congregation, and we must also participate in a group within that life of the whole congregation in which we seek to understand the meaning of our commitment to Jesus Christ and the implications for our life as colonists in the world.

This has an interesting parallel in the book of Acts, where the early Christians were reported to spend their time as follows: "And day by day, attending the temple together and breaking bread in their homes, they partook of food with glad and generous hearts." (Acts 2:46.) These are the two foci of our life as Christians about which I am speaking. We join in congregational worship. We meet in small groups. We must dare to involve ourselves in some form of a small unit within the life of the church, where we are in fact face to face with our fellow Christians and in which the relationships of understanding, trust, and love have some chance to grow.

I am saying this against the background of the communities in which most of our church members live. The church is no longer the expression of a natural human community. In America, at least, and I think abroad, the parish concept has virtually been eliminated. We live dispersed and not in a colony. When we come to the church for our corporate worship on Sunday morning, we may, even though the church is small, be a gathering of those whose lives have not touched each other during the previous week. We do not live in natural, human communities where we know each other in Christ and where, during

58

are really colonists in the world, they find themselves so battered and bruised from the conflict and the toil that they come to corporate worship with a tremendous sense of need and urgency. The sacramental life of the colony takes on a power that is compelling. This is not a book on worship, but I would mention here a few principles that have made a significant difference to the East Harlem Protestant Parish.

After a great deal of experimentation we are a little startled to find that we have come up with a fairly traditional Reformation order, which involves considerable congregational participation but also seems to us to say something quite specific and appropriate in the course of the unfolding worship pattern. I am persuaded that the situation in East Harlem has not primarily determined the elements of worship in any localized way, but rather these suggestions are easily applied elsewhere.

1. The reading of the Scripture and the sermon belong together. The Bible is open during the early part of the liturgy, but following the *initial* section of the service, the minister picks up the Bible and carries it to the pulpit. He then reads the scripture, including both an Old and New Testament passage. With the Bible still open on the pulpit, he preaches a sermon based upon the scripture read. Wherever possible the preaching follows a pattern through a number of weeks, usually being related to the Bible study in which the congregation is currently engaged. Not only am I making the point here that the reading of the Bible and the exposition of the scripture belong together, but that also there is tremendous advantage when the congregation is aware of the pattern of the preaching during the particular time of the year and is engaged in study and consideration of the passages either before or after the sermon itself.

2. The climax of every authentic service of Christian worship is Holy Communion. In a sense every Sunday morning service of worship is a Communion service but is cut short before the final reception

of the bread and wine. Thus we have felt it appropriate to begin the service of worship behind the Communion table, giving there the call to worship as an invitation to unite together again in worship around God's table. The offering, appropriately, is the beginning of the specific service of Communion and thus rightly comes after the preaching of the Word. On Communion Sunday, after the money offering is taken, the bread, wine, and money are then brought forward together in an offertory procession and together placed upon the table. On Sundays, when we do not have Communion, the offering still follows the preaching of the Word, as a symbol of our response to what God has done in Jesus Christ made known to us anew in the sermon. It thus serves as a reminder that the service normally is complete with Communion.

3. The service of Holy Communion. In large churches the mechanics of Communion are serious obstacles indeed to a real sense of fellowship around a common table. Our congregations, for better or for worse, are sufficiently small that we can actually gather in a circle around the table. Even when this is not possible on a particular Sunday, the elements are passed out quietly while the congregation joins in a hymn. We then take the bread together and then the wine. At least to this degree we are able to eat and drink together as a symbol of our unity around Christ's table.

4. Special services. In almost every case baptisms are performed as part of a regular service of public worship and not as a private matter, either in the church or in someone's home. Wherever possible marriages are also placed in the context of a service of worship, though at a special time. People in our parish now feel that they have not really been married unless the service involves the singing of hymns, prayers, the reading of Scripture, and a sermonette, as well as the service in which, before God, the couple exchange their vows.

C. *The Content of Our Common Life*

There is something further to be said about the wineskins of our common life in the church. If we accept as valid the conception of the two foci, we must still be concerned not only with revitalizing our forms of worship but also in discovering concretely the pattern of life for the time we spend together as Christians apart from corporate worship. The second chapter of the book of Acts, the forty-second verse, provides a clue: "And they devoted themselves to the apostles' teaching and fellowship, to the breaking of bread and prayers." At the risk of sounding like a biblical literalist, I would submit that we deviate from patterns of the early church at considerable peril. We can rationalize greatly about the changed times, but increasingly I am persuaded that the church that takes seriously its missionary character will discover that in the experience of the early church there are patterns for our life today of indescribable value. In a quite fascinating critique of the missionary movement, written many years ago but recently reprinted (*Missionary Methods, St. Paul's or Ours?*, World Dominion Press), Roland Allen argues convincingly that when the church does not take these patterns seriously, it is in very great danger. He makes the point that in actual fact the missionary tasks of the church in the twentieth century has more parallels with that of the first century than with any other era of Christian history.

Whether this be true or not, I would suggest that Acts 2:42 does suggest the pattern for what we might well do as absolute essentials in our life in the colony. Assuming the corporate worship of the church on the one hand, the four aspects of our common life which we dare not escape are these:

a) *Apostolic Teaching*. I take this to mean the study of the New Testament and in a larger sense the history of the Christian church. If as Protestants we really do take seriously the centrality of Old and New

63

Testaments, then our biblical illiteracy is preposterous. We shall not overcome our ignorance at this point by telling people they should read the Bible; rather we must undertake together a long-range, steady, plodding approach to this business of our ignorance. For a number of years now I have been involved in Bible study at least on a weekly basis and also required to read a daily lectionary. There are encouraging signs that my own biblical illiteracy is at least being partly alleviated by this consistent reading of the Bible and regular study of substantial parts of it.

It has been most exciting in our parish to see what can happen when a group of laymen are involved in Bible study for a consistent period of time. For example, at the Church of the Ascension during the past two years the members of the congregation were asked to make their small group involvement through Bible study, meeting in various homes throughout the housing project in which nearly the entire congregation resides. Many of the church members responded by inviting into their homes for these meetings those who were uncommitted to the church or frankly skeptical. During one three-month period the first letter of Paul to the Corinthians was the subject of our Bible study. By the time it was over, we had all been through a tremendous experience that had opened our eyes to the parallels between the struggles of our own congregation in the middle of East Harlem and that of the little church in Corinth in the first century. We had come to know each other on a far deeper level and had begun to be honest about our real commitment to Jesus Christ. Often after the Bible study would break up, the discussion which it had initiated would go on until midnight. Logically enough, the preaching of the church for this period also was taken from First Corinthians, which meant a real unity between the Bible study groups and the preaching of the word on the following Sunday.

In East Harlem we also publish a lectionary for each section of the church year, designed for use in people's homes in family or individual devotions. Wherever possible the Bible study will follow the lectionary as another way of unifying our study efforts.

A good deal has been written about methods of Bible study, with particular thanks to Miss Suzanne de Dietrich whose works are increasingly being translated into English and should be familiar to all of us. She rightly emphasizes the difference between the corporate study of the Bible in which we really seek to stand under its judgment with our brethren and its use for private devotions. Both are important, but they are complementary and neither should be avoided.

"Apostolic teaching" can, of course, apply to much more than Bible study; but again and again we are discovering that it is in the context of the small group that real teaching can take place, for it is there that people expose the points of their genuine concern and ignorance.

b) *Fellowship.* I presume this means simply that when Christians come together, they are concerned with one another. Here we have a chance to discuss how the battle is going in the world, to find comfort and strength from one another. The primary point to be made is that when as Christians we come together in the life of the church, it is not to carry on a conversation that has no point of contact with our oneness in Jesus Christ. If our gossip in the church is the same as our gossip over the bridge table, we might as well stay at the bridge table.

One interesting experience in our Parish may illustrate this point. The Asbury Methodist Church, a fine church in Westchester County, was interested in helping their Christian brethren in East Harlem. Out of our mutual relationships came the suggestion that their laymen and ours have a weekend retreat together. It was very interesting as the planning for this joint venture developed. I got the distinct impression that both the East Harlem laymen and those from Asbury were equally worried about the outcome, both being a little afraid and uncertain in the presence of the others. We arrived on Friday evening at a retreat center owned by the East Harlem Parish and sat down around the room to get acquainted. The inevitable suggestion was offered that we go around the room and tell who we were. Had this been done in secular fashion it would have been all the more disruptive, for the worldly positions of the Asbury group were quite notably in contrast to the group from East Harlem. However, someone quickly offered the suggestion that in going around the room we simply give our names and then tell why we were Christians, this obviously being the only thing we really had in common. As human beings the differences in our education, interests, and culture were tremendous. God makes us very different, but we had only one point where we stood completely together. This was in our relationship to Jesus Christ. It was quite a memorable experience, as one by one each person in the room attempted haltingly, sometimes almost pathetically, sometimes movingly, to indicate how he had been led into God's church. In the process, if those present from Asbury will not take offense, I would submit that the group from East Harlem seemed to be a good deal more knowledgeable and certain of what their pilgrimage had been. The procedure broke the ice, and for the rest of the retreat the laymen wrestled with concrete ways in which they must express the Lordship of Jesus Christ, both in the church and in the world. Cultural differences have a way of becoming quite insignificant when we face our task as Christians and let our unity in Christ be the center around which our attention is focused. When we demand that Christians take time from their mission in the world to spend it within the protection of the colony, it is crucial that this time be used with good stewardship and faithfulness to our Lord.

c) Worship. For the early Christians worship in the homes was primarily the receiving of the Lord's Supper. This was truly a celebration of the messianic banquet, a reminder of the life to come in a kingdom of which this was a foretaste. Here in some sense, but with great reality,

66

Jesus Christ was present and entered into their bodies as they were bound anew to his body. It is significant, I think, that wherever I have been inspired and caught up by a sense that some genuine renewal was taking place in the church, it is a fact that Holy Communion is a very central act of that community. Communion is celebrated weekly, if not daily. We Protestants, in so many denominations, have let the Sacrament become a quarterly or monthly matter, on the assumption that it is about as much as people can take, that if we had it more frequently it would lose its meaning. There may be some validity in these objections, but I think they rather point to the obvious fact that this very central aspect of the life of the Christian community has slipped away from us. Communion no longer, in fact, is an expression of the reality of our life together through which we are caught up again into the power of God in Christ. But this was the case for the churches in the New Testament, and it is becoming true again for many Christian communities in our day. It was true for the worker-priests in Paris; it is true in the Iona Community. In East Harlem we have begun to have communion on a parish wide basis every Sunday morning at 8:30.

One of the most significant statements about Holy Communion comes from Canon Ernest Southcott, an Anglican in Leeds, England, in his book, *The Parish Comes Alive*. His name is associated with the "house church movement." Canon Southcott recognized some years ago the tragic separation of the sacramental life of the church from the actual life of men in the world. Taking the second chapter of Acts seriously, he has developed a plan by which every morning, before men leave for work, the Sacrament is celebrated in homes of various members of the parish. It is a moving experience for those who have gone with one of the priests of the church into the home of a workman at 6:30 in the morning and sat around a kitchen table where the family and friends have gathered. There the Bible is read and the Communion is offered, using the bread that will later be eaten at the breakfast meal. Here the church is moving out of the sanctuary into the world where it belongs. The Sacrament, which is a reminder to us that it is our daily life which we offer to God, then is received as men go off to engage in their daily tasks. The spiritual reality expressed through the physical makes the whole into a transforming experience of our unity.

d) Prayer. Finally, the life of a Christian group is a life of prayer, and prayer in the form of intercession. It is in intercession that we look outward to the world. We bear the burdens of other men before God, the concerns of our life "out there." This is not some sentimental identification with those in need but our continual reliance upon the grace of God. Because we know that God is faithful and that God's love endures, we dare pray for our fellow men. Because in Christ God has given us the freedom to bear one another's burdens and the capacity to love those in need, we dare pray for them.

Intercession, therefore, has nothing to do with persuading God to do what men would like to do; it has no part either of self-inducement, bolstering men to do what they want to do. Intercession has nothing to do with men's will for themselves, but only to do with God's will for the world. NEVERTHELESS, NOT MY WILL, BUT THINE, BE DONE. Intercession is the freedom of Christians to suffer with and for others as a witness to the world that in His suffering for the world, God has overcome suffering. Intercession is a celebration of this good news for the world, which is, at the same time, of course, God's will for the world.[1]

In a small group our prayers can be quite concrete. We pray not for the starving people "somewhere" but for the people whose lives have touched ours, who are hungry or in need. We pray by name for the lady next door and the boy down the street who has been hurt. We

[1] William Stringfellow, "The Christian Lawyer as Churchman," *The Christian Scholar*, Sept. 1957 pp. 222-23.

pray for the things that are real for us. We are personally involved in what we are doing and saying.

Thus, in our common life, we are called together for fellowship, for study, for worship, and for prayer. In all of these it is the mission of the church which must be our central concern, for it is thus that we express our obedience to Jesus Christ. The enabling group and the corporate life of worship must prepare us to go back in obedience and faithfulness into a world where God has placed us as his witnesses.

In all of this I am not attempting here to outline some ideal situation in the church but rather to argue that there are concrete structures which can be brought into the life of our church through which it may be possible for the Holy Spirit to shape our lives anew. As Bonhoeffer, in *Life Together,* so strictly warns us, we have no right to set up an ideal and then demand that God grant it to us. But we do have the right to begin wherever we are in openness to offer ourselves to our fellow men and seek new wineskins with others who have declared that he is their Lord. For all the dangers which any particular structure may have, for all the reservations which people may have against this kind of argument for a cellular structure within the life of the church, I am persuaded that it is of desperate importance that we begin to take a step or two in this direction. It is far better to take a step cautiously but firmly than to spend our time arguing about the errors into which we may fall ten steps further down the road. The danger of too much worry about this is that we take no step at all.

CHAPTER IV

THE MISSION OF THE CHURCH
I. The Witnessing Community

> As therefore you received Christ Jesus the Lord, so live
> in him, rooted and built up in him and established in the
> faith, just as you were taught, abounding in thanksgiving.
>
> Col. 2:6-7

The task of witness has traditionally been defined as evangelism. This is a word I wish to retain, if we may consider evangelism as all those ways by which Christians witness to the reality of God in Jesus Christ and thereby make known his power and love to the world. Evangelism is the Church's concern that men be called from darkness into light, that men who do not know the truth about the world discover the secret wisdom of God, that men who seek to live by their own wisdom find the power and the foolishness of the gospel.

In this and succeeding chapters we shall consider evangelism under the headings of community, service, and proclamation (in Greek, *koinonia, diakonia, kerygma*). We begin with the witnessing community, the fellowship of the church. For I am persuaded that in the depersonalized world of the twentieth century, it is the very life of the colony which will confront the world with the power of the gospel. The world needs desperately to see love in human relationships, to see harmony between men of incredible human differences, to see peace amidst the most fantastic chaos and disruption. By its very existence, without doing anything other than being a community of God's people, the colony witnesses to the gospel.

human backgrounds can share together the meaning of their new life in Jesus Christ in which they have been given a new humanity that makes them brothers.

Equally important is the witness, which the world cannot overlook, when a local congregation cuts across racial divisions and proves the inclusiveness of the gospel. The failure of the church at this point has been more noteworthy than its success.

But here and there Christian congregations are proving, beyond a shadow of a doubt, that in Christ racial barriers can be overcome. Often they stand against the mores of the community. I am persuaded that in East Harlem our churches would have grown far more quickly had we been willing to appeal to one racial group rather than to seek always to reflect the racial composition of the community. All our natural human disposition drives us not into integrated churches but into segregated ones, whether it be along class or cultural lines. Is it not right that we pay the price of fighting against this human disposition for the sake of the gospel? Clearly when a church does stand fast and in its life brings together people of different races, the world does not ignore the witness. It may not like it; it may argue against it; but it is challenged by a concrete confrontation between the gospel and the values of men which may, by God's grace, lead men to Jesus Christ.

B. *The Witness of Our Mutual Concern*

Bear one another's burdens, and so fulfil the law of Christ. . . . For each man will have to bear his own load.

Gal. 6:2, 5

The mutual love and concern which typifies the life of the Christian colony again is a striking witness to the world. In our day and age there are few people so protected from the realities of human existence that they are not aware of the insecurity of human life. A woman moving into a new housing project in East Harlem is caught between two conflicting desires. On the one hand she is afraid to get involved with her neighbors for fear of the demands they will place upon her, but at the same time she knows she must quickly find some neighbor whom she can trust in case of trouble in her own family. Whether it be the people of wealth seeking out their psychiatrists or the people of poverty asking the help of social workers, a vast number of people in our day are clearly in need of help in meeting the demands of life.

In the Christian community we are called upon to bear one another's burdens and thus fulfill the law of Christ. The trouble with most of us in the churches is that we simply do not know our brethren well enough even to be aware of their problems or needs. Again and again it is in the context of relationships created by the small group that we really are permitted by another person to be aware of his needs and thus fulfill the opportunity which God has placed before us. Then for the first time many in a congregation can be involved in a net-work of relationships of love and concern, which is a reality of tremendous witness to a world tormented by its own insecurity. This is the central meaning of the doctrine of the priesthood of all believers.

One trouble quickly arises in nearly every congregation. This has to do with the role of the laity, a matter which we shall discuss at greater detail later. Here the point to mention is the way in which the average layman expects the clergyman to be the one who is the primary burden bearer for the congregation. When someone has a real spiritual problem in the average congregation, it never occurs to him that anybody but the minister could be of help. The clergyman is the paid specialist in this area. But if I read the New Testament correctly, Paul expected that in an ordinary congregation some person would be gifted as the preacher, but others would be gifted as healers and pastors. I suspect that within any congregation with which any person reading this book is familiar, there are people who by their sensitivity and compassion have clearly been singled out by Almighty God to be the pastors of the congregation, with potential pastoral capacities far exceeding those of the clergyman, in spite of all his courses and summer clinical training. The clergyman's task is to recognize and encourage those so gifted, even if it means denying himself the satisfaction of being the focus of the counseling for the whole congregation. The priesthood of all believers will become a reality.

It is also important to note that in our world, in which the ability to bear another person's burden so often is presupposed to demand considerable professional training and competence, the result has been a rather considerable impersonality. It is the church which must keep alive the reality of love for another person, for love genuinely offered is more powerful in meeting the real needs of most of us than a great deal of technical skill. This is not to enter into an argument with professional social work but to keep in proper perspective the unique quality of life and the incredible power released by a congregation in which mutual concern is expressed.

One other obvious point about the witness to the world which can be made by a congregation in which this kind of concern is mutually expressed. When the whole life of the congregation depends upon the minister, the resources are far more limited than when a congregation is made up of cells whose members have come to know one another in depth and who for each other release the sources of God's love. The possibilities are instantly multiplied.

C. The Witness of Our Dependence Upon the Holy Spirit

In him, according to the purpose of him who accomplishes all things according to the counsel of his will, we who first hoped in Christ have been destined and appointed to live for the praise of his glory. In him you also, who have heard the word of truth, the gospel of your salvation, and have believed in him, were sealed with the promised Holy Spirit, which is the guarantee of our inheritance until we acquire possession of it, to the praise of his glory.

Eph. 1:11-14

A Christian fellowship is bound together by the Holy Spirit. A congregation of Christians come together on Sunday morning ostensibly in the expectation that by the power of the Holy Spirit new truth and new light will break forth in their midst. When Christians gather for study and discussion, it is with the assurance that wisdom and direction will be given to them. But let us be honest, the reality of the Holy Spirit is almost unknown to most of us who go by the name of Christian. Whereas Paul speaks in very concrete terms about his experiences of the Holy Spirit and obviously is referring not to some theological doctrine but to very concrete and specific encounters when he was gripped by a reality that changed his life. Most of us would be hard put to it to define our most recent encounter with the Holy Spirit. Perhaps this is quite directly related to the protection which is now offered to us by the present structure of our congregational life. Occasionally, through the preached word the Holy Spirit may be able to break into our lives, but this does not as frequently happen in our day as in ages past.

Rather, I am persuaded the reality of the Holy Spirit for most of us will primarily be known when we are finally willing to expose ourselves to steady and consistent periods of time with fellow Christians, where together we are seeking to face the implications of our life in Christ. In this situation we are willing to be honest with one another, to listen, to be judged and corrected by our brethren. Is not this in very fact the way in which the Holy Spirit will touch most of us?

For myself, whenever a decision of importance is confronting me, I must take seriously the biblical injunction to go into my room and pray. I find that I can struggle with myself for a long time and after real anguish of soul arrive at a course of action which I have persuaded myself is God's will for my life. However, I am under a discipline which commits me to discuss vocational decisions with a group of fellow ministers. Not infrequently, when such a hard-won decision is exposed to this group, I discover that within a few moments they have been able to reveal, in a loving and concerned way, the unconscious self-deception in which I had indulged. It is quite apparent that I have endless capacity to deceive myself into deciding that what God wants me to do is in line with what I really want for myself. But in the context of fellow Christians, whose judgment you trust and who have no ulterior motive but to assist you, it is difficult to avoid the honesty which God expects of us.

This is simply my way of saying that for me the reality of the Holy Spirit has again and again come in the context of the Christian community through other people. God somehow doesn't seem able or want to break through to me with a clear and unambiguous voice, except as it comes in this way. And for most of us who are comfortable, middle-class Christians, living in America, the word which comes to us from our brethren is almost certain to be an uncomfortable or a judging or a demanding word. It is a dangerous thing to expose ourselves to the Holy Spirit. When we are gripped by the Spirit, the point of view from which we view the world is radically changed. Now we are called upon to see life through the eyes of faith and not from the human point of view. We seek to discover God's will for us and not to impose our will upon God. The relationship of unity with my brother and concern for him is confirmed.

To avoid ever putting ourselves into the kind of Christian community where the Holy Spirit can get at us is a sure way of making life a lot easier and of deceiving ourselves completely about the nature of the life in Christ. The witness of Christians impelled by the Holy

77

Spirit is foolishness to the world, and yet it gains a hearing. In the midst of its insecurity the world is startled by men who live with confidence and joy.

D. *The Witness of Our Transcendent Loyalty*

I appeal to you therefore, brethren, by the mercies of God, to present your bodies as a living sacrifice, holy and acceptable to God, which is your spiritual worship. Do not be conformed to this world but be transformed by the renewal of your mind, that you may prove what is the will of God, what is good and acceptable and perfect.

Rom. 12:1-2

The final witness which can be made by the life of a church comes in the way in which it prepares its members to live with Christ as Lord in the midst of the world. The true colonist is a person operating in all he does on behalf of the Lord of the colony, but I am persuaded that only when there are cellular units within the life of the congregation will men really be able to express to their brethren the problems which they face in the world and thus enable the church to prepare them for their witness in the world. People are tired of hearing ministers urge them to be obedient in their business relationships and faithful in their witness through the Sunday morning sermon. The words spoken, the demands made sound so completely out of touch with the concrete reality of the decisions which they must face. The pulpit degenerates into "ideal mongering" that is a source of great frustration or despair, for the Christian lives in a world that is not black and white. We cannot preach a message and then leave people, in isolation, to work out its implications. Within the life of the church people must find concrete help in facing the problems of the world in which their life is placed, the concrete orders of work, family, and politics. They must discover specific help in what they are to do in these settings

78

and what form these obligations must take upon them. Without this the preaching of the church will consist of empty recommendations to piety which leave the world to its own fate.

Members of a church live in concrete historical situations. When they are permitted or required within the life of the church to consider these various specific situations, then they may in fact become colonists who take seriously the implications of their obedience. The church must address very firm and positive demands to its members in terms of the concrete situations where they live in influence and responsibility. This is to say once again that the message of the gospel is concerned with the entire life of man, that is, with his *whole life* and not merely with his soul abstracted from the evil world. In its life together the church must be concerned with the battle of the colonist against the principalities and powers of evil and his endeavors to witness to Jesus Christ in his daily life.

The tremendous importance of the life of the *koinonia* as a witness to the gospel is perhaps summed up in the word "demonstration." By its very life the colony is called upon to demonstrate the reconciliation which has taken place in the gospel. The world wants to see and feel and taste the reality of God's love and of the salvation which has been granted through Jesus Christ. The church is the city set on a hill, the lamp on the table, by whose rays the world is confronted with the light of Jesus Christ. When the gospel is lived and its fermenting power made visible in the actual life of the congregation, the world is sharply confronted with the necessity of a decision between light and darkness.

CHAPTER V

THE MISSION OF THE CHURCH

II. The Service of Men

> But Jesus called them to him and said, "You know that the rulers of the Gentiles lord it over them, and their great men exercise authority over them. It shall not be so among you; but whoever would be great among you must be your servant, and whoever would be first among you must be your slave; even as the Son of man came not to be served but to serve, and to give his life as a ransom for many."
>
> Matt. 20:25-28

The concern of this chapter would, in most churches, be seen at once as the province of the Social Action Committee. In most alert churches there is almost certainly a committee of those people who happen to have a particular interest in the application of the "principles of the Bible" to the problems of society, or who recognize that somehow the gospel is supposed to be relevant to the problems of human society and are seeking to find means by which they can express their concern. Too often this is simply one committee made up of those who "like that sort of thing," while those interested in evangelism find themselves on another committee. Perhaps these aspects of the work of the church must be administered through such committees, but almost inevitably they bespeak a real distortion and limitation that is quite false to the gospel. The work of the church is mission. The business of the church is thus, in the broadest sense, evangelism. What I am here calling the service of men or social action is a vital aspect of the mission of the church, for it is in this way that we demonstrate both the love of Jesus Christ for the world and the willingness of Christians to fight against the principalities and powers of evil in his name.

The key word is "servant." As the Lordship of Jesus Christ was established by his willingness to be a servant of men, so the Christian can only hope that the authority of his Lord will be established if he too becomes, in actual fact, the servant of men. To become a Christian, indeed, means to change one's vocation. However one earns his daily living, whether as lawyer, teacher, housewife, artisan, or student, as a Christian his primary vocation is that of servant. Every task to which we set our hands must be done in the light of this primary vocation. In Germany, after the war, in the course of restoring a great cathedral, amid the rubble was discovered nearly intact the lovely statue of Jesus Christ which had stood in the front of the church. The only missing pieces were the hands. The sculptor indicated that he could quite easily replace the hands if the congregation wished. After some discussion it was decided that the statue must be placed back in its position of honor with the hands still missing, as a constant reminder to the congregation that in the world where God had placed them they must indeed be the hands of Jesus Christ, and through their lives and witness must be expressed his concern for every problem that limits and warps human life.

A. The Location of Our Service

The metaphor "colony of heaven" also illuminates the nature of Christian service. The colony exists for the sake of the world which lies outside its protecting walls. His business, of necessity, takes the colonist outside the walls and into the midst of the place where men live in ignorance of the Lord of life. For a long time the church, with some justification, has been able to relate itself primarily to the geographical place where men lived. But as man's residence and place of work have been separated, the church has found itself cut off from the arena in which the forces that determine much of modern life are operative. In our day men as likely find their basic community in their place of work or leisure as in their place of residence. It is rather uncomfortable to discover that the church is identified with the residence community but completely cut off from the world in which men work, some number of commuter miles or subway stops away. The clergyman, as the men go off to work, stays home with the mothers and children in his pleasantly circumscribed religious ghetto.

But the purpose of the colony is nothing less than to "be there" in the midst of the real world, wherever men live and work and play. Only in being there can the colony hope to serve men at the point where their needs, frustrations, sickness, and fears emerge. The colony must intrude itself in someway into those places where men are living out the deep concerns of their lives.

One of the most exciting developments in recent years in the Christian world has been the worker-priest movement in France. With the permission of their bishops a few priests put on the clothes of the worker and obtained jobs in factories, working side by side with the people. They discovered anew what it was to stand with their brothers, to learn again to speak the language of the man in the street, and to face the frustration and boredom of a large factory. At night they would come home from their work to a slum apartment and there, in the robe of the priest, celebrate mass on the kitchen table. Their evenings were spent in a life of service through which they sought in every possible way truly to express Christ's love for men. The church had gone out there because people would not come in to the sanctuary on the corner, the ugly, unfamiliar, and rather foreboding bastion of what too often seemed an alien culture.

It is a hard thing for the church to pay the price of "being there" in the complicated world in which we live. It has been a real struggle for Protestantism to face the estrangement of the inner city areas of our great cities and realize that we must almost begin over again in terms of witnessing to our gospel in vast sections of Detroit, Cleveland, Chicago, New York, Los Angeles, and the rest. In recent years we are beginning to wake up to the problem, but certainly we who have worked in East Harlem would have to confess, with very deep chagrin, that we have only begun at best to understand the problems of the colony in such a community and have made little progress in the light of our commission.

Part of the problem is that the world is suspicious of the colonist. He is an intruder who has suddenly arrived in the new land with some kind of material motive or imperialistic claim. It was very trying for the young clergy of East Harlem Protestant Parish in 1948 to discover how unwanted they really were by the community. Several times the clergy were mistaken for plain-clothes detectives or numbers men. Somebody sidled up to one of the staff and said out of the corner of his mouth, "Hey Bud, what is this? A new racket of Mark's to get ahold of the people?" ("Mark," Vito Marcantonio, was then the left-wing congressman from East Harlem.) In a community which is predominately made up of minority groups a white face is almost automatically under suspicion. A white face may be a landlord, owner of one of the lousy tenements, a narcotics peddler, a gambler, or one of the professionals who come to "service the community."

More noticeable than the suspicion or the occasional antagonism of the community, is the sheer weight of apathy. When the colony arrives, it is to proclaim the gospel that is both very new and very old. There are few people whose lives were not at some time touched by Sunday school or church. The words of the New Testament are not unfamiliar; day by day on the radio or TV, preachers of one kind or another shout the old familiar words about sin and salvation.

But most people have long since stopped listening and have decided they have heard it, and for their own reasons reject the gospel. Even the colony must itself exhibit new wineskins, must be there in some kind of new way if it is to build any kind of bridge from its beachhead into the world.

I remember well as a young clergyman, calling on all the families in a tenement building. Several months later I was stopped on the street one warm afternoon by a tall Negro who said, "Hello, Brother Webber." I obviously didn't recognize him, and he explained that I had called on him in building 311. I looked up the call later on my cards and discovered that we had talked only for half a minute through the partly closed door. I had told him a little about the church and left. But he had remembered my name these months and then said, "You know, after you left my wife said to me, 'Reynolds, you old good for nothing, we've lived here in this lousy place twenty years, and all kinds of people have knocked on your door. They've all come here to get you into trouble, to get your money, or to go out and get drunk or to sell you drugs. That's the first time a good man ever knocked on your door.'" The fact that God's church had not been there for twenty years gave Mr. Reynolds the right to wonder whether we were serious. The beachhead could only be established when there was some sign of caring, when the church made it clear that it was there out of genuine concern.

The world may seek to keep us out, but as often the colony fails to go out into the world in ways that indicate much sincerity. It puts a sign on the door saying, "Everybody Welcome," but in effect is offering the concern of the Christian community only to those who come to it. If people will come on our terms, then they are welcome. In every possible way the church must really go "out there," for it is outside the church where people live in the midst of their problems. There we must be with the love of Christ as the unique power to which we point. Or in subtle ways we offer the resources of the church as a way of saving our own institutional neck. An example is the church in a changing neighborhood that finally welcomes minority groups only out of desperate need to keep the church doors open. Or we too easily slip into the habit of helping people "because they are poor and needy," rather than because they are really like us, people for whom Christ died. Our paternalism or unconscious sense that we have been made better or superior by Christ stands in our way.

For me this has been a recurring problem in my ministry. It has been all too easy to develop a fine theology of social justice and to work hard in the battle and yet find it very difficult to feel that the often unlovable victims of injustice, one by one, are my brothers in Christ. I am sure that only a church truly filled by the love of Christ and speaking through men and women in whom he lives is able to take the colony there where the need of the world is found. It is easy to affirm that in Christ all men are one; it is another matter to be empowered by the Holy Spirit with real compassion, to feel in one's heart love for one's parish, to have patience with the ugliness of life, to hope in the face of tragedy and pain when one discerns no hope. Even now it remains difficult to face the realities of our community, to stop our theologically sophisticated romanticizing and come to honest identification through full participation in the life of the community. Such new forms as the store front church or the insistence that our clergy live in the community achieve nothing unless through them is expressed this spirit of *being there* in the midst of God's world.

B. The Weakness of Our Service

In the course of its whole history the church has taken with great seriousness the story of the Good Samaritan. This and the stories of healing by Jesus and his disciples have been symbols of the compassion and service which the church has rendered to men in all ages.

Wherever the church has gone, it has healed and educated men, taught them the meaning of freedom and human dignity, fought against fear and superstition. Most of the great educational institutions of the west, as well as our hospitals, have roots within the life of the concerned Christian community.

In America the church has often been the conscience of society. It has been Christians who have glimpsed a problem which warped or twisted human life and initiated a crusade against it which frequently has had significant consequences. But today we live in a much more complex situation. In the face of the vast problems of our society, which we have described under the general heading of depersonalization, it is no longer possible to apply the story of the Good Samaritan in any very direct way. Much of what the church attempts in the way of service in our day is superficial and perhaps naïve. The witness of our service grows weak when we misunderstand our brother's need or offer only a palliative.

The naïveté is symbolized by the problem of the white gift service in the Sunday school at Christmas time. We have been a little startled in East Harlem in recent years to recognize how serious a problem this is for some churches. In order to teach the little children that Christmas is giving as well as receiving, the Sunday school has a white gift offering. After the lovely pile of gifts has been presented (I am afraid sometimes purchased on Saturday afternoon by mamma and dutifully wrapped up in a way that hardly gets across to junior the principles involved), somebody says, "My goodness, what do we do with them now?" Apparently some Protestant churches are not even sufficiently in touch with their community to know where the gifts can best be used. At that point someone remembers having heard of the East Harlem Protestant Parish and sends the gifts off to us. The amount of gifts which are received in our parish are a very mixed blessing. Incidentally, we have learned to deal with the problem they created by turning the problem over to the laymen of the Parish. The gifts are unwrapped and divided into groups at a penny, nickle, and dime level. We then have a mammoth toy sale in each church to which the parents of our children and others in the community are welcome to come and, at a very nominal amount, purchase their own gifts for their children. In this way some of the implications of the power of the clergy to call manna down from heaven are overcome. But my point is that some Protestant efforts to help our needy brethren really do become as naïve as this.

Perhaps it is also part of our Protestant heritage which leads people to suspect or assume that those who are poor or in the grips of some tragic problem, like narcotics addiction, are really somehow at fault. Occasionally, after I have described to a women's group the problems of East Harlem, someone will say to me words to the effect, "I hate to hear you talk about East Harlem—what a terrible place to live. But, of course, there are plenty of jobs these days; people wouldn't have to live that way unless they wanted to, would they?" When one recognizes the handicaps and limitations placed upon a youngster born in a tenement in East Harlem, in his struggle to realize and fulfill the potential which God gave him, one certainly cannot use the word "blame." There are vast forces in our industrial society which dominate and thwart his life and are completely beyond his control. We must be careful about using the image of the free individual whose destiny is in his own hands or fall into the Christian heresy of assuming that in this life God has blessed the successful and damned the alcoholic and drug addict. I often get irritated at the tones of paternalism, self-righteousness, and condescension with which my fellow Christians in East Harlem are treated by their more middle class brethren. I, too, am all too easily trapped by my heritage as part of that vanishing breed in our large metropolitan centers known as Wasps (in case you haven't heard, white Anglo-Saxon Protestants).

Most of the parish staff face the obstacle of being white-faced and middle class to the core. We were shocked at the appalling living conditions in the tenements, the incidence of narcotics addiction, and all the social problems that beset the inner city and confounded our middle class ideas of what America was like. When the staff families moved into the community to live, they found that simply who they were created barriers that had to be recognized in order to have any hope of surmounting them. It was very difficult, in spite of all our intense desire, to see our parishioners as brothers for whom Christ had also died, men and women who, in spite of the adversity in their lives, were in God's sight as worthy of salvation as we.

Again, the service of the church often has sought superficial solutions to really serious problems or has been unprepared to deal with the actual facts of the power of politics. When Protestants resort to political action and speak a prophetic word by standing above both political parties, they may simply have made themselves odd man out. In the face of some serious community problem Protestant ministers or groups are likely to issue a strong statement to the press. The Catholic priests are more likely to go around and see the local politicians and get some changes made. In traveling around the world, one of the staff of the World Council of Churches recently said that the most distressing discovery he made was to see the great concentration and deep concern of missionaries in almost every land he visited and yet to recognize their complete lack of training that would enable them to understand the dynamics of social change taking place all around them and with which they had no choice but to be concerned.

The remarkable little phrase used frequently by Bishop E. R. Wickham, for over fifteen years an industrial chaplain in England, points to the heart of the problem, "the *secular relevance* of the *Gospel*." All three words are important. The Christian must not only understand fully the meaning of the gospel; he must also know about the secular world in which his life must be lived in order that the relevance of the gospel may be communicated. We dare not concentrate either on knowing the world or knowing the gospel or on means of communication, but the three must be bound indissolubly together if the secular relevance of the gospel is indeed to be a fact in our time.

One other area among the many issues with which the service of the church is confronted is that of the old argument between the church taking action in society and Christian individuals who have been converted then changing the institutions of the world. There is somewhere a fallacy in this argument that ought to be apparent in the kind of world in which we now live. Individual Christians, operating in the world, rarely have any sense of support and direction from their faith which enables them to do anything whatsoever about changing the basic structures of life in modern industrial society. It may, in fact, not be possible for a denomination or a church to take much direct action in society or on many occasions to speak a prophetic word to the world. But this does not preclude the life of a denomination or congregation from being continually directed toward the problems of which men and women are confronted in our world and seeking through its common life to give to individuals the kind of support and direction which enables them to work at points of importance for social change.

This is venturing too far into territory thoughtfully and carefully traversed by the ablest professors of Christian ethics, though perhaps part of our problems lies precisely in this fact. Excellent thinking has been done about the problems of social ethics, but far too few actual attempts have been made by Christians to take seriously the implications of what the professors have had to say. At the risk of theological superficiality, or even heresy, Christians in our time must be about the business of demonstrating to the world the relevance of the gospel. I only suspect that this will be done in a variety of ways and not by any one approach. Certainly in different situations the church as church must act, whereas at other times it will be individual Christians identified as such who will struggle with the problems of their community. At other times the Christian must join with quite secular groups in working together at a common task. Most frequently in a city like New York one discovers that when he engages in a struggle for justice, his support and strength come from secular people who seem to possess greater sensitivity to human needs than he. God offers us many channels by which we may serve him. We must be alert to use these new wineskins.

C. The Content of Our Service

1. THE LOVE OF CHRIST, FREELY GIVEN

The content of our service is the love of Christ, poured out freely wherever there is human need. Whatever the wineskins by which we seek to serve our brothers, the only thing we have to offer is Jesus Christ. That fact alone distinguishes the work of Christians from all others who seek to help their fellow men.

No Christians ever have to look far to find those who stand in need of Christ's love. Around every church, whether it be in the slums or suburbia, live men and women whose lives are broken or captive or filled with anxiety, whatever their economic situation may be. Whenever a church, through its ministry of service, offers its help, there is always far more to be done than its resources permit. People often come with their desperate human problems, wanting to know if God's church offers any hope. More often we must go to them if they are to be helped.

Shortly after the beginning of the parish we took as our purpose the words read by Jesus in the synagogue at the beginning of his ministry:

> The Spirit of the Lord is upon me,
> because he has anointed me to preach
>   good news to the poor.
> He has sent me to proclaim release to
>   the captives
> and recovering of sight to the blind,
> to set at liberty those who are oppressed,
> to proclaim the acceptable year of the Lord.
>
> Luke 4:18-19

Apart from the gospel every man is captive or blind or oppressed or poor. Many men have some suspicion of their condition. They seek hither and yon for release or sight or riches. Often they will test the church. People who have never seen love in action, people who assume that the world is against them, people who have suffered and been betrayed must test love in action for a long time before they will trust it. One of the most painful aspects of the ministry is to be tested—to have the kids break in the doors and steal from the church, and in every possible way try us to see at what point we will reject them.

Nor dare we have as a direct motivation for our social concern to find ways of bringing people into the life of the church.

The church cannot look to the preservation and maintenance of its own life if it is to be an instrument of Christian witness among delinquent youth in American cities. Clergy and laymen must look outward at the streets and people around the church asking not "How can we relate these people to our church?" but "How can we relate ourselves and Christ's Gospel to this place and to these people?" [1]

It is always a temptation to subordinate social action to evangelism

[1] From letter by George Todd in *Christianity and Crisis*, March 31, 1958, p. 43.

rather than to see the witness of love as itself a sign that points directly to Jesus Christ. The social work of our churches is often regarded with suspicion by people. It seems to be simply a means to an end. If we are only trying to fill our empty churches, it is wrong. The New Testament commands us to love our neighbor as the whole fulfillment of the law. This is subordinated only to our love for God. We do not love in order to convert. Love loves for its own sake; it loves in order to help the other person. How right it is for a church to find that it is giving far more of its time to those who show little sign of commiting their lives to Jesus Christ than to those who are already members of the church! Christ's love is always freely offered.

But at the same time it is not the church's major task to join in every humanitarian effort to improve the lot of human life. We are not "professional do-gooders," but the task in which we must be engaged is clearly defined by our function as a colony. It is easy to dissipate our energies in all kinds of peripheral and unrelated efforts to "help others" in a way that is not our business. The crucial work of the colony is always a sign which points, in however partial and broken a way, to God's kingdom. It points to the saving work of God in Jesus Christ and must be an analogy to Christ's own ministry. "This special service of the church has to be *a help of the helpless.*" [2] It is the special function of the church always to be on the alert and to pray to God that she may really see the helpless people of our day and then have the courage to take up the task of service which is demanded.

At the same time we live in a society in which increasingly governmental and private agencies are taking over much of the humanitarian service directed toward the helpless that previously has been the province of the church. We must have the courage to give up these

[2] Hendrikus Berkhof, *The Church's Calling to Witness and to Service, Christian Century*, October 16, 1957, p. 1,227.

tasks when they are no longer our business. When the helpless have been discovered and are being assisted by other organizations, they no longer are the special object of the church's ministry. When others are able to do as well or better particular tasks undertaken by the church, it has lost its significance as a service which points to the restoration of life in Jesus Christ. There are tremendous gaps in the services provided by secular agencies. The church must be there sensitively and humbly offering her resources.

It is an obvious fact in American life that most of the problems which warp and limit human life, which create helplessness in men and women, can most effectively be dealt with through political channels. Here lies the path of relevant love. The naïveté of Protestants about politics is overwhelming. Politics has even been identified as the real source of evil in American life and is something which good Christian people too often avoid with a real sense of superiority. Can one not on the contrary argue that to be a Christian citizen in a democratic society makes participation in politics an absolute necessity? We have no right to be the odd man out, avoiding responsibility for the structures which make our common life in the world possible. Furthermore, much of our service degenerates into sentimentality if we do not seek to use the channels of political life.

Don Benedict, the first full-time clergyman of the East Harlem Protestant Parish, was standing on the corner of 104th Street and Second Avenue in East Harlem one afternoon when a coal truck raced through a red light and in the process knocked an old man down in the gutter. The instinctive response was to pick the man up and rush him to the hospital, but the requirements of our society demand that an ambulance be called and that one express his instinctive desire to be a good Samaritan by calling for help and making the man comfortable until the government provides the means of conveyance to proper medical care. Don did this and then sat by the man for an hour and thirty-seven minutes awaiting the arrival of the city ambulance.

In thinking about the episode afterwards, we recognized how the obvious desire to be a good Samaritan in our society has been made so much more complicated. The only way really to fulfill the biblical injunction would be to get better ambulance service for East Harlem. The only way to get better ambulance service is to put pressure on the local political boss and ultimately on city hall. But you have no pressure to exert unless you and those who feel as you do have been actively engaged in the political enterprise.

At perhaps no other point has the ministry of the East Harlem Parish been so strenuously criticized as that of its political involvement. The clergy do not preach politics from the pulpit or tell people how to vote, but they have come to the clear conclusion that as citizens in our society they have not only the right but the duty to participate actively in the political life of the community. Since East Harlem is a one party situation, to limit one's political participation to voting in the regular elections is to take the way of complete irrelevance. The political realities demand that one become a member of the party, able to vote in the primaries, and find ways of becoming involved relevantly in the actual decisions of the local political boss, who by the way, in East Harlem or anywhere else, will welcome with no enthusiasm the participation in the local organization of any group of citizens about whose ultimate loyalty to the party he has any doubt. Responsible participation in local political life does open channels of pressure and influence which can be of very great importance in making some small progress against the frustrating problems of an urban community.

Our concern with politics seems strangely placed under the heading "The Love of Christ." But the two are linked in our complex society. Our calling to love our neighbor must be more than service to those

94

individuals whose need confronts us. For the sake of the individual Christ's love constrains us to strive to change society, in fact, to colonize the world. We must do battle directly against the principalities and powers of evil which still seem to rule with such dehumanizing and enslaving power. In the illustration of the Good Samaritan it is not enough to deal with the problem of the man beaten by the gang of thieves. If the Good Samaritan happened to be a commuter journeying daily to Jericho, he would have been a little fed up with having to spend some time every morning dealing with the latest victim of the gang of thugs. After a while it might occur to him to do something about the problem of police protection along the road. So the Christian, faced with the frustration of dealing with the victims of injustice, is led to do something about the structures which create these problems. George MacLeod of Iona reminded us once that it was blasphemous merely to pray for a little girl who had contracted TB in an East Harlem tenement and see that she got good medical care. God demands more than this. We must, as Christians, do something about the rotting tenement in which other little girls are threatened with TB.

When one looks around for examples of churches or even Christian individuals who consciously have engaged in this kind of struggle for social justice, one finds tragically few examples. It is obvious, through no virtue of its own, that in a community such as East Harlem the church has been free to engage in such a struggle. Here, when the church fights for better housing or better schools, it is working in the clear self-interest of its own members, and if it has any virtue, it is a virtue not its own. For many Christians, to work for social justice in concrete patterns would seem to go against their own self-interest and clearly lead them into conflict with their neighbors. If the Christian in a suburban community sells his house to a Negro, he faces a quite different situation with his own neighbors than does the Christian in East Harlem who joins with others to form a tenant's association in a public housing project.

At the beginning of our ministry we were confronted with the fact that in East Harlem there was a high incidence of drug addiction. The addict was often rejected by his family or the fact of his addiction hidden from public view. About 1951 we decided to let the community see something of the grimness of the problem and the fact that the church was aware of the living hell of drug addiction. An able young writer named Maryat Lee was commissioned to write a play called *Dope*. This was presented to the community on a makeshift, wooden platform on five different vacant lots in the community. It was a most remarkable experience for everyone concerned, but its primary purpose was to dramatize the evil of addiction to a good many thousand people. From that time on a steady stream of addicts and their families began to turn to the churches of the Parish for help. Our help was almost nil. No one has any real clue as to how to help the drug addict. The only resources of our society are institutionalization in the federal narcotics hospital in Lexington, Kentucky, for addicts over twenty-one, and in recent years, a hospital for teen-age addicts run by the City of New York on an island in the East River. In spite of the dedication of the staffs of both these places the incidence of cure is fantastically small.

By the fall of 1956 the dimensions of the problem were something that the Parish could no longer overlook, and we felt that a major attack must be launched against this evil. The primary challenge came from a couple of young laymen who kept reminding us of all the sermons the ministers had preached about the relevance of the gospel to human need. One minister was assigned to give at first part-time and eventually full-time to our work with addicts and their families, supported by a remarkable committee of laymen, including some professionals from outside the community, ex-addicts, and some of our own church members. During the twelve months of 1959, 511 new addicts came into the little narcotics headquarters in a store front on 103rd Street. They entered under a simple sign on which a large cross is shown smashing into pieces a glass hypodermic syringe. This dramatic sign expresses the faith by which the Narcotics Committee works, that only through the power of the cross can the evil of addiction be defeated. The ministry of the Narcotics Program is concerned not only with helping the individual addict to face his problem but in developing new legislation, in pressure upon city authorities for more adequate medical facilities, and the general effort to awaken the public to the seriousness of this problem. The program is expensive, the results meager; but in the face of this situation which society has virtually ignored, the church seemed to have no choice but to do the best it could.

A very striking witness in the church's effort to witness in the world against the power of evil comes through the Iona Community in Scotland. During the depression years, George MacLeod, already a great and famous minister of the Church of Scotland, grew terribly concerned that in a time of poverty, depression, and misery the churches seemed to have no word to say but were struck dumb by the problems of their day. He resigned from the large church of which he was pastor in order to assume the ministry of a church in the middle of a poor section in Glasgow, amidst the unemployed. In 1938, he was responsible for founding the Iona Community, a fellowship of clergy who are seeking to find patterns by which the relevance and power of the gospel can be made known in our industrial society.

The ministers of the Iona Community, although they are under regular appointment to parishes in the Church of Scotland, have bound themselves together by a discipline regulating much of their life. They have become a source of great inspiration to people all over the world.

97

One of the central emphases of the Iona Community has been the concern for the relevance of the church in the world. Again and again MacLeod speaks of the necessity of the church to move from its religious ghetto back into the market place. The church must discover again a way of living in and for the world. He has a story about a church in Scotland where, under a great stained glass window, were the words "Glory to God in the Highest." One day a boy threw a stone and knocked out the "e" in the word "highest." He pointed out how true the phrases had then become, "Glory to God in the high st (reet)." Both phrases need to live side by side. We give glory to God in the highest precisely by the way in which we live on high street. God is only glorified if we are living in concern and compassion on the streets where men live "out there."

2. THE ASSURANCE OF VICTORY

In this entire chapter we have been alluding again and again to the present Lordship of Jesus Christ as though this were something that is readily taken for granted within the church. The colony is a proper wineskin only if it does demonstrate the reality of Christ's rule over the world. It is in our service that this witness is made. But here is an area of great misunderstanding in Protestantism today. In our serving we affirm that Jesus Christ is Savior. We seek to offer his saving love to men, praying that they may come to know the meaning of salvation. This emphasis is a true one, but unless it is balanced by an equal emphasis upon the present Lordship of Christ over the world, it quickly degenerates into a distorted version of the gospel, which carefully circumscribes the "sector of our religious needs" and is concerned only about saving souls out of the evil world. The church becomes a refuge from the world so that even in our historic Reformation churches a strong sectarian principle has entered in. To say that Jesus Christ is Lord of the world means almost nothing to the average

Christian. To understand our service in the world in the light of this affirmation means nothing at all.

It is not very easy, however, for any of us to express what this really means in a way that can be communicated with much success. What sense does it make to say to the people of East Harlem that Jesus Christ is Lord of the community, that in spite of the exploiting landlords, the gangsters, the numbers men, the narcotics peddlers, the crowded tenements, the cold impersonal services, and the discrimination, the world looks different through the eyes of faith, for Jesus Christ now has established his rule?

I am sure that our problem has also been complicated by the historic role of the social gospel in American Protestantism. I happen to have been brought up in a church where the burden of the minister's preaching and prayers had to do with giving our lives to bringing in the kingdom of God. To me this was accepted as a quite possible goal. The kingdom of God would be achieved if and when enough Christians worked hard enough at the task. There was work to be done, goals to be accomplished, and when we had given enough of ourselves to the task, the world would indeed be clearly seen as a better place in which to live and the kingdom of God would daily approach nearer. This may sound naïve, but it does reflect an attitude prevalent in some Protestant circles. It is a very dangerous business to determine for ourselves the ways in which the kingdom of God will be achieved on earth and all the more dangerous when almost inevitably it means that we must have some concrete and visible signs that progress is being made.

Recently a beloved older friend in the ministry took me aside with some deep concern. He was afraid that after a few years in East Harlem I would end up bitter and cynical. He explained that through the course of his life he had known many young men who had seen some serious human problem and with some courage and with considerable energy had set about fighting the problem. He indicated that again and again he had seen them end up bitter and discouraged after years of struggle, for the results of their work were meager, and the problems seemed rather intensified with the passage of years than brought under control. He was fearful that the same thing would happen to me.

Clearly, this is a possibility that may lie ahead for any of us, but one can only respond that the motivation for the Christian's work in the world is to bear witness to the present reality of the Lordship of Christ and not to bring in the kingdom of God. We work in the foreknowledge of the kingdom of God, participate, even though dimly, in the life now through our involvement in the body of Christ, the colony, that over the hostile, antagonistic, and apathetic wilderness in which our colony is set the sovereignty of God has already been claimed and that the land is owned by our King, even though the present inhabitants are unaware of this fact. We are there to speak about the King, but the fact of his kingship has already been established. This alone is what makes our servant life in the world possible. We can live and fight against the principalities and powers of evil with confidence. Jesus Christ is Lord. This is the central truth of the gospel. This is the hidden and secret wisdom which we know and which we deeply wish to share with the world. God has given us the protection we need for our warfare.

Therefore take the whole armor of God, that you may be able to withstand in the evil day, and having done all, to stand. Stand therefore, having girded your loins with truth, and having put on the breastplate of righteousness, and having shod your feet with the equipment of the gospel of peace; above all taking the shield of faith, with which you can quench the flaming darts of the evil one. And take the helmet of salvation, and the sword of the Spirit, which is the word of God.

Eph. 6:13-17

I asked Marcus Barth, author of the excellent book on evangelism, *The Broken Wall,* based on the study of Paul's letter to the Ephesians, how one might get this truth across in some way. He suggested the analogy of the American Army troops on a remote Pacific island following the signing of the peace treaty on the deck of the battleship "Missouri" in Tokyo Harbor. The battle between America and Japan was over; a victory had been won; a peace treaty had been signed. But on the island the Japanese troops had not gotten the word. They were still fighting with deadly concentration. The American soldiers assigned to the thankless task of the mopping-up operation could just as easily be killed then as before the peace treaty was signed; yet even at that moment they could not but live in the sense of the reality of a time when peace had come, when for their own families the world was different.

This does point to something of the truth about the world at the present moment. In the life, death, and resurrection of Jesus Christ something new did take place that was decisive both for individual human life and for the world. The power of evil in the world has in fact been broken; a victory has been won; a peace treaty has been signed. Jesus Christ is Lord. It is our job as colonists to live as those who know that the peace has been signed and to testify to the reality of the new Lord. This is why for the Christian no defeat is possible. This is why Paul can write the eighth chapter of the book of Romans and testify in such power.

For I am sure that neither death, nor life, nor angels, nor principalities, nor things present, nor things to come, nor powers, nor height, nor depth, nor anything else in all creation, will be able to separate us from the love of God in Christ Jesus our Lord.

Rom. 8:38-39

This is why the Christian can face the ambiguity of political involvement and take the risk of the errors that inevitably follow upon the need for decision and involvement. This is why the biblical metaphors for the church are not that of a triumphant army, by its own strength bringing in the kingdom of God, but rather the quite different figures of leaven and yeast. The Christian is called upon to find, or perhaps simply to accept, the place of servanthood in which God has called him and there to live in the reality of the kingdom, which both is and yet is still to come. Whether he succeeds or whether he fails in his particular job, if he has done all in his power, is in God's hands. He is content to leave the verdict there, where it belongs. God expects of him only faithfulness in fulfilling the servanthood that has been given to him. For those who have accepted their servanthood, it is this knowledge alone which enables them to continue in the face of the bitter battles of our life. For those who have not yet accepted the servanthood of Jesus Christ, this kind of talk may simply provide another way of escape. Someone said to me recently, "Those are dangerous words to speak in America, for you too easily assume that you have accepted your servanthood, when in fact you are still living by the lordship of your little gods." But truly to live as a servant is to share the life of one's master, to follow Jesus in a path that may involve suffering, rejection and conflict and yet leads ultimately to joy, love, and peace.

CHAPTER VI

THE MISSION OF THE CHURCH

III. The Proclamation of the Gospel

> Now the eleven disciples went to Galilee, to the mountain
> to which Jesus had directed them. And when they saw
> him they worshiped him; but some doubted. And Jesus
> came and said to them, "All authority in heaven and on
> earth has been given to me. Go therefore and make dis-
> ciples of all nations, baptizing them in the name of the
> Father and of the Son and of the Holy Spirit, teaching
> them to observe all that I have commanded you; and lo,
> I am with you always, to the close of the age."
>
> Matt. 28:16-20

A. Preliminary Issues

1. THE RELATION OF SERVICE AND PROCLAMATION

Evangelism means witness to Jesus Christ. In the sense in which we
have been using this word, it describes the mission of the church. The
church has borne witness in different times and places in many different ways. There are occasions when dynamic action in society is called
for; there are other occasions, perhaps clearly evident in our day, when
the simple presence of a worshiping community witnesses to men of
our God. There are other times when a word must be spoken.

I have purposely placed the speaking about Jesus Christ, the proclamation of the gospel, the kerygma, at the end of this discussion on the
mission of the church. It is no less important than the other two.

Service, the life of the Christian community, and preaching are inextricably bound together; to take them in isolation is to distort the gospel. But, precisely, this isolation seems to me the serious threat in terms of present patterns of evangelism in the United States. We have spoken too often when we should have been silent and been silent when we should have spoken. When one listens to the incredible amount of preaching that comes over the airway and on the television screen, one suspects that men and women have long since ceased to be challenged by the words and phrases in which we talk about the great events in the gospel and are merely bored.

The very nature of the church requires that the witness of the church through the spoken word and the witness of the church through acts of service and love must always be kept together. On the one hand the church, through its inner life, represents the beginning of the kingdom; while on the other hand she is the herald who points to the kingdom which is to come. A church which simply talks about the gospel without a life of love and service has no convincing power. When she talks about the reality of God by which she is not herself possessed and which she does not take seriously, she will not herself be taken seriously. At the same time it is impossible to imagine Christians whose only calling is to serve and for whom this occasion never gives an opportunity to speak of the mighty acts of God. Such a church or such a Christian would be without compassion, for the very men whom we serve above all else need to know the saving power of Jesus Christ. Nothing we can do, however strenuous our works of mercy may be, will be sufficient to deal with the ultimate problem of human sinfulness or provide the ultimate ground for peace and hope.

In considering the relation of service and proclamation I have been helped by the story of the paralytic man, as it appears in the gospels. In this dramatic story a man with a serious human problem, the physical illness of palsy, hears about a faith healer in a nearby town and is taken there by his friends in the hope that healing might take place. When the man is finally brought into the presence of Jesus, by being let down on his pallet through the roof, Jesus looks at him and then instead of healing the palsy tells him that his sins are forgiven. Presumably, this not only upset the enemies of Jesus who were present but also rather frustrated the poor victim of palsy, who had not come to hear about his sinfulness but to be healed of his disease. To him Jesus must have sounded much like the typical preacher, whose solution to all human problems is simply believe in Jesus Christ and everything will be "okay."

In the Gospels Jesus, as proof of his power, looked at the man then and said, "Arise, take up thy pallet and walk." The man's palsy was healed, but far more important, through his desire to find a solution to his quite real human problem, he was confronted with his ultimate need. Presumably, like any victim of poverty or illness or injustice, he had certain bitterness in his heart, but more important, as a human being he shared in the universal problem of our sinfulness, our self-assertion, or alienation from God. Through this confrontation with Christ he was led to recognize that beneath the immediate problem which had brought him into the arena of Jesus was a much more ultimate problem of which he was not then aware.

The healing and the forgiveness do not stand in opposition to each other, but confirm each other. Healing is the sign of the reality of the restoration of human life which comes through Jesus Christ. The healing ministry of the church in service and in the struggle for justice always points to the reality of Jesus Christ. We always pray that through our freely given service men may also be confronted with the deeper need of which they are unaware. The people who, in our day, seek the ministry of the church come not out of a deep sense of sinfulness but because of some human need for fellowship or purpose or healing. God gives us the opportunity now and again to provide them with community and healing. We must be alert so that when the opportunity comes, it may also be an occasion through which they may come to recognize their ultimate need for the forgiveness offered to us by Jesus Christ and the acceptance of their responsibility to serve him. In one sense it would be far easier for men to deal only with the palsy or only with the problem of forgiveness. The sect churches of East Harlem seem primarily concerned about man's need for forgiveness. The secular social agencies seem only concerned about the problem of the palsy. It is the task of the true church to live in the tension of both, giving its energy to the problem of palsy as fully as it gives its energy to speaking about the gospel. These two never dare be separated.

Early in the history of the East Harlem Protestant Parish a group of men and women from the very poor tenement building next door to the first store front church came to see Don Benedict to say that for several days they had had no heat in their building. The landlord, trying to save money, had set the thermostat located near the oil burner at 50°. As a result the families in the building had been without any heat whatsoever during a very bitter December week. This had happened a number of times before, but the tenants had been terrified to make any protest. Even now it had taken considerable courage to come and ask Don if there was anything he knew they might do. He suggested they get the facts by each getting a thermometer or two from the ten cent store and for the rest of the day keeping track of the temperature in their rooms. They were to return the following morning. The temperature readings, when produced the next day, were a pretty sorry picture. Don at once called the city Department of Housing, and, before he could be shunted off to some other department, told the bureau that the tenants were all on welfare, would all certainly come down with pneumonia, and would cost New York a great deal of money if they didn't get an inspector up right away. For whatever reasons an inspector did come up that very day, and after taking a look at the thermometer readings, he set the thermostat at 80°. Shortly thereafter a summons was issued for the landlord to appear in court. It was a great day for the tenants when they and the minister together went to court to stand up before the judge and testify to the injustice to which they had been subjected. A kind of self-respect and integrity seemed to have been granted to them at last. However, on the way out of court one of the men said to Don, with real bitterness and considerable sadism, "This is really terrific. We've got that old so and so over the barrel now. We're really going to make the landlord suffer."

In a very real sense the church had been helping the tenants face a problem of their palsy. Now had been developed a relationship between the minister and this man which at least enabled them to talk at a new level of comradeship and understanding. In a direct way the man had poured the bitterness and hatred in his heart out where it could be seen. Now that the manifestation of palsy was beginning to be dealt with, the underlying problem of sinfulness, in its form of bitterness and hate had been exposed. Now there was a real opportunity for the ministry of proclamation to begin as a result of the ministry of healing which had taken place.

2. THE QUESTION OF CREDENTIALS

In its provocative documents the Division of Evangelism of the Study Department of the World Council has raised a number of important questions with which the churches of our time are asked to concern themselves. One of these has to do with the "credentials" which the world demands of the church for the authority it claims to possess. A minister in East Harlem set out to call on all the thirty-three families in a tenement building. To his knock on the door comes the inevitable response, "Who?" and the door remains barred. In this and every other way the world asks the church for its credentials.

Who are we to knock on every door and what validates our authority to those inside? The world has every right to ask this question, but too often, in its eagerness to win the world, the church gives the wrong answers or short-circuits completely the process by which it would maintain its own integrity. The primary credentials which a church can possess are simply to be the church, to reflect as fully as God makes possible the being and life of the people of God. In the world this can only show itself when the church, through its members and its own life, expresses the servanthood of Christ. "For what we preach is not ourselves, but Jesus Christ as Lord, with ourselves as your servants for Jesus' sake." (II Cor. 4:5.) When the church, by the mercy of God, is the servant of Christ and does its work in the spirit of a servant, it possesses the only possible credential.

There is deep need for repentance in the face of the failure of Christians to accept the form of a servant in their dealings with their fellow men. We have not in fact permitted Jesus to put this distinctive form upon us. In the face of our failures we need again and again to return to him as the only source of our renewal. No matter how hard we try, we can never be certain that we are servants of Jesus Christ. But his demand is ever upon us, judging, calling, reminding, and sometimes empowering us. When, as in the case of Jesus himself, the world is faced with those who live as servants, there is an inherent authority that cannot be argued or proved but has either to be accepted or rejected.

In all areas of social concern, including involvement in politics, we must never forget that our credentials lie not in our success in changing the world or overcoming evil. Our only hope is to live in the world by God's grace and thus expose to the world the real meaning of evil, the true facts of the human situation. We are witnessing in the world to something we already know about what God has done. In the degree to which we reflect this new reality and not in the degree to which social improvements are made are we faithful to our commission. When God gives us grace to labor with this perspective, to be faithful in the face of discouragement that is real and defeat that hurts, then sometimes the world does respond.

So many times now people ask us why. Why do we keep up such a hopeless fight? Why do we not leave when so few people listen? Why do we work with addicts when everyone knows that they are hopeless? Is this not the means by which the way may be opened for the word of God to be preached and received? Over the years it has often been in the context of social action that the evangelistic question has been posed. Now the world initiates the question. The secular lawyer wants to go home and talk all night about the basis for our involvement with him in a common battle. Above all, when behind the Christian in his work in the world there stands the fellowship of the church, he then can invite men into a community where what he is talking about has begun already to come true.

In spite of this men may ask for signs as they address the question of credentials to Jesus. Sometimes God does give signs, even as Jesus pointed out to the disciples of John how the sick were healed. In our day the sick will also be healed; prisoners will be visited; lonely men will find comfort; light will shine in the darkness. But what signs do come serve not as proof for credentials; they only point to God and his presence with his church. They may open doors of communication. When new health does come or a new job or a better apartment or any other modest human joy, this must be used as in the story of the paralytic man to speak to the person about the ultimate problem of all our lives. In serving, we earn the right to speak. God can thus use our witness in his own way to speak to our neighbors.

And then there is the task in which no signs come at all. The Narcotic Program of the East Harlem Protestant Parish illustrates this. The minister in charge has been related to almost one thousand individual addicts. To date he can report only a handful of cases of arrested addiction, but God has given him and his colleagues this work to do, and so they labor on. Where continuing our task depends on signs, they may tempt us to forget the faithfulness of God.

3. THE QUESTION OF INTRUSION

What authority do we have for intruding into other people's lives? The only response of faith to this question is: We do not intrude. The doctrine of creation has, for me, become the key to this matter. God made us in his mighty act of creation. The world was good and under the dominion of man. But man, in the disobedience of the fall, shattered the wholeness of creation. "Therefore as sin came into the world through one man and death through sin, and so death spread to all men because all men sinned." (Rom. 5:12.) Man was the intruder who disrupted the work of creation. But God cares about his world. He never rejected the Israel that rejected him. He sent his Son into the world to call us back into the reality of life, into the kingdom. Thus Paul speaks of Christ as the New Adam who died for us. He entered into a world broken by man's intrusion with his promise of the restoration of creation. We live in the period between the entry of God in Christ into the world and the conclusion, between the promise and the fulfillment. The evangelist, therefore, does not intrude but, rather in urgency and faith, announces to men what God has done for them.

In our ministry in East Harlem there was another issue in the matter of intrusion. This has to do with differences of culture and education. From the beginning we were able to look upon our neighborhood as our parish. There were no competing Protestant churches. Everyone in our area was looked upon as a parishioner. As a missionary venture we were clearly an intrusion into the community, moving in as neighbors in the tenements, knocking on every door on a whole block, and in general entering into the life of the area. It was hard not to violate the integrity of the hearer by our intrusion, for the clergy tended to have resources of all kinds that put him in a privileged position. The temptation has always been, in subtle ways, to overwhelm or dominate, to cajole or entice those to be evangelized. It is an equal temptation to look through eyes predominantly focused by middle class standards and values and not by the gospel. Clearly, these dangers of a false intrusion are great and perennial.

But for us the evangelistic task meant that we must seek to reveal to men the reality of their own lives and not point to ourselves. It is for us to try and open up eyes that are blind to the true predicament of sinfulness, so that men would stand naked in their need before God. Then they might in truth be able to accept the Lordship of Christ, or to reject it. The evangelistic question would be posed. The addict, in his bondage, tried to insulate himself from life. The woman next door, as she moves into the new project, announces, "I ain't going to bother nobody, and I don't want nobody to bother me." To both the evangelist is an intruder, an annoyance. But we know that there is no privacy; there is no escape; there is no way out for men from meaninglessness and anxiety and death, except in Christ. Ahab sees Elijah as an intruder, "Is it you, you troubler of Israel?" And Elijah answers back, "I have not troubled Israel; but you have, and your father's house, because you have forsaken the commandments of the Lord and followed the Baals" (I Kings 18:17-18). The evangelist challenges the world with the same response. His authority, in this sense, is related to creation. It rests upon the faithfulness of God, revealed supremely in Jesus Christ.

4. THE QUESTION OF URGENCY

It is perhaps blasphemous to discuss the urgency of our task, when we should be fulfilling God's command and not debating it. Unfortunately, we are sufficiently confused about the urgency of our task that some sense of direction is needed. No longer are we satisfied with the urgency of an earlier generation to "save souls from damnation."

We hesitate to suggest that the salvation of another depends upon our work or to predict the judgments of God. Nor do we seem to be energized by the knowledge that we live in the period before the Second Coming, when the sheep are to be gathered in. Nor are we motivated by the assurance that every man will stand one day before the judgment of God. But a faithful church seems always endowed with an overwhelming sense of urgency in its mission. Wherein does this imperative lie?

Urgency is the reflex of our relationship to Jesus Christ. God is a missionary God who in Christ has come into the world to save it. The urgency of our task lies in the very nature of the gospel event. The Christian is one whose life has been grasped by God's action and who knows that his life now must be lived in order to reach out to all men everywhere, claiming them for their rightful Lord. When we have felt Christ's love, we "naturally" seek to point others to the same love. It is an incredible gift we only possess in sharing.

5. THE QUESTION OF AUTHORITY

In this task our only authority is found in absolute acknowledgment of the faithfulness of God and our dependence upon his grace. In East Harlem we have learned that neither our enthusiasm nor our bright ideas for social action, nor our moral purity, nor our compassion for the brokenness of East Harlem were of much avail. We had no authority on human terms. We were humbled under the mighty hand of God, humbled in terms of our confidence in all our plans and methods and theology; and yet the one clear task is that of mission. In this situation the words of Peter took on a new reality.

Humble yourselves therefore under the mighty hand of God, that in due time he may exalt you. Cast all your anxieties on him, for he cares about you. Be sober, be watchful. Your adversary the devil prowls around like a roaring lion, seeking someone to devour. Resist him, firm in your faith, knowing that the same experience of suffering is required of your brother-hood throughout the world.

I Pet. 5:6-9

So for the church the battle always rages. The adversary is very real. In the midst of it now and again we recognize our authority, affirm again, in spite of pride and self-reliance, our dependence on God. In Jesus Christ the faithfulness of God has been made known to us. The God who revealed his name to Israel now comes to us in his son, and now we know what the faithfulness of God really means. It is under-stood at the foot of the cross. It places us continually there at the point of the cross, in the places of crises and need and brokenness, for this is the real situation of man. Our dependence is not on our solutions nor even our faithfulness, but upon the faithfulness of God and the miracle of the resurrection.

The reality of this confession is known only in rare moments when God has driven us not only to know but to feel with our whole being what it is to live by his power, to be a new man in Christ. To live by his power is to be an evangelist, not as a specialized task within the church or even within the particular province of the clergy, but as the work of every Christian. There is, then, no separation between work and worship. To worship in praise and thanksgiving and in-tercession is to lift the whole of life up to God. To live in the world in witness, judgment, and service, is also our spiritual worship. "Woe is me if I do not preach the gospel," is an authentic response of every Christian.

B. The Goal of Evangelism: Obedience to Jesus Christ

In this discussion of contemporary evangelism we are obviously mak-ing several assumptions which must be made clear. What are we after in evangelism? Are we seeking the kind of conversion in which

113

a man accepts Jesus Christ as Lord and then, following this rather traumatic and earth-shaking experience, is left pretty much on his own to work out the implications? Are we seeking primarily to incorporate people into the life of a local congregation? Or is it that we are seeking people who will join us in the good causes for which we struggle in Christ's name? Clearly it is all of these.

D. T. Niles suggests that conversion must always involve three aspects of a man's life and that our obedience to Jesus Christ is complete only when all three have in fact occurred. Clearly, a man must accept Jesus Christ as his Lord and Savior. But there is no meaning in this unless it is in the context of the Christian community in which his life is then an integral part and by which he is sustained and nurtured in a continual study of the meaning of his commitment. Finally, this obedience to Jesus Christ must be expressed by his vocation in the world. As we said earlier, a Christian changes his vocation and becomes, in his whole life, determined by the fact that he is part of Christ's body to be a witness in every moment of his life. In every way his commitment to Christ must impinge upon the decisions and patterns and even habits of his daily life. Someone has said that when a person is truly converted to Jesus Christ, it means that his instincts are different. Another said she hopes that through her life of faith, increasingly her habits will reflect the gospel. It is imperative that one see these various aspects that are involved in saying that one truly has committed his life to Jesus Christ. All three, the acceptance of Jesus Christ as personal Lord and Savior, participation in the life of a congregation, and obedience in daily life, are crucial if Jesus Christ is truly to be Lord and Savior.

The significance of this to the evangelists and the evangelizing church is clearly that the point of entry to a human being may be at the point of any one of these three aspects of obedience. D. T. Niles tells the story of a mission in which he was involved some years ago in India. He and a group of evangelists had gone into a small Indian village to preach the gospel. After a week the village chief came with his leaders to say that the whole village was to be baptized—several thousand of them. Nile's colleagues were appalled at the idea and affirmed that such an action was really impossible. "How can one baptize a whole village when they obviously know nothing about the Lordship of Jesus Christ?" Niles, however, insisted that the step was appropriate. Why did these people wish to be baptized? Because in the brokenness of India, in the midst of the caste system they had seen the love and power of the Christian community, and they wanted to be part of such a group. Niles said, "We must baptize them and then within the life of the church they will be confronted through the preaching of the Word with the Lordship of Jesus Christ and trained in obedience for their life in dispersion in the world."

He told this story at a conference on evangelism attended by most of the secretaries for evangelism of the major denominations in America. It was interesting to see the reaction of the people in the room as this story was told. It seemed a wonderful illustration for precisely what we are doing in America today. We are baptizing a great hoard of middle-class Americans, who come to us and want to join the church. We know they are ignorant about the Christian faith and faltering in their obedience to Jesus Christ. Our theory is that once they have joined the church, we will then have an opportunity to convert them, exactly along the lines that Niles indicated. You could see this reaction going through the minds of the people in the room, many of whom were busy writing this story down as a good illustration for their next speech. Before they put their pencils away, however, Niles spoke up sharply, and I believe I quote him correctly.

Let me make one thing emphatically clear. This illustration has no relevance to your situation in America. You are not dealing with people who have caught an authentic glimpse of part of the Christian life, nor do you baptize them into churches where they will be confronted with the Lordship of Jesus Christ but into social clubs.

This suggests that in presenting the gospel there are methods which seemingly are successful but are incongruous with the gospel itself. The nature of the gospel sets certain limitations which we must not transgress.

1. The gospel must be so presented that the person accepts some really integral part of its message of what God has done for him. We have no right to permit people to say that they accept Jesus Christ as Lord or are prepared to participate in the life of the Christian community if they have in fact not a glimmer of what such promises mean. It is far too easy in our day to get people to make such promises precisely because the life of the average church is so flabby.

2. The integrity of the person must be respected. We have no right to override the conscience of a man or to use any methods which manipulate or depersonalize him.

3. The decision must not be so posed that a man can say "yes" without being required to complement this with some specific obedience. Our presentation must be concrete. Faith and obedience are inextricably bound together.

4. People must not be invited to accept a faith and then told that the second step is to join the church. To accept Christ as Lord is to be part of his body, the church. Genuine conversion is, in some sense, always an aspect of the life of the Christian community. It is the church through which God makes known his message of salvation in Jesus Christ and in no other way.

Another way of putting the problem is to say that we must not permit people who commit themselves to Jesus Christ and his church to remain in a spectator role. They must not be permitted to say "yes" intellectually and then avoid the consequences. Too often the careful church membership class, which precedes a person's entry into the church, is looked upon as a course from which one graduates and in effect becomes a Christian alumnus for the rest of his life, his education complete and he is now free to sit back and criticize the administration.

C. Experiments in Evangelism

Here and there across the world there have been arising, in the last several generations, exciting signs of renewal in the life of the church. A kind of instinctive comradeship and unity emerges whenever the men and women from these situations gather to discuss the meaning of their faith and the mission of the church. For the American church there is great value in becoming familiar with the Taizé Community in France, the struggle of the worker-priests in Paris, the insights for the service of the church developed by the Kirk-en-Wereld in Holland, the ministry of William Gowland, a Methodist industrial chaplain and pastor in Luton, England, the experiences of the churches in areas of rapid social change around the world, and many others. One of the most helpful functions of the evangelism section of the Study Department of the World Council of Churches has been to keep in touch with these often lonely pioneers and to send out information about the various signs of renewal and experiments in evangelism which are taking place in Christendom. Here I will mention three or four places where signs of real encouragement are to be discovered in the light of our concern in this chapter on proclamation.

1. NON-CHURCH CENTERED:

ESTABLISHING COMMUNICATION WITH THE WORLD

In America the concerns of the church have usually been relegated into a kind of a religious sector, and men who believe they are committed Christians are able to compartmentalize their life in such a way that their obedience to Jesus Christ has no implications for their life in the world. In the European scene, on the other hand, the world has simply decided to ignore the church, under the conviction that the gospel has nothing to say about the really important matters of the world and human life. In the face of this deep alienation there have been a number of attempts to bring the church back into conversation with the world, in order that there might be channels through which the wisdom and relevance of the gospel might be brought to bear again on the problems of the world. In Germany, with some similar developments in other countries, there has been a very extensive development of what is known as the Evangelical Academy. This emerged shortly after the Second World War, out of a sense of real desperation within the German church. The religious life of Germany had been largely paralyzed by the effect of Hitler; now it was important that the church take itself out of its ghetto existence into the life of the world. The plan developed had no immediate implications for strengthening the church itself through bringing in new members, but was concerned to establish a point of contact between the life of the church and the life of the world. The spontaneous response to the early Evangelical Academy programs led to the development of eighteen such centers, one in nearly every section of Germany, including several behind the Iron Curtain.

The Academy serves as a neutral ground where vocational groups are brought together for serious discussion about the particular problems of that location. For instance a group of trade-union leaders, with the blessing of their companies, meet for three days of discussion, not about the Christian faith but about the concrete problems facing trade-union leaders in Germany. Some of the leaders would indeed be committed Christians, but a great many of those who came were not. Economists and political scientists, as well as theologians, served as leaders. There were no holds barred as the group sought to look at the concrete ethical problems which they faced in their day by day work. The theologians and other Christians present had to take their chances with everybody else. Here was a real testing for the church. If in fact our biblical faith provides a frame of reference which makes sense out of human existence, it had a chance to be expressed.

Out of a concern to re-establish communication has developed the work of Ted Wickham in Sheffield, England. For sixteen years, until his recent election as a bishop, he directed the Sheffield Industrial Mission. Recognizing the estrangement of Protestantism from the workers in the Sheffield factories, he has tried to re-establish contact. He would affirm that one cannot communicate the content of the gospel until one is in communication at the level of common human concerns and interests. Wickham and his able staff, usually numbering about seven clergy, have won real acceptance from both labor and management over the years. The engagement is entered into at the level of what Wickham calls "the secular relevance of the Gospel." In sessions, after work or at tea breaks, groups of men gather to discuss the issues of central concern to them—from management practices to the hydrogen bomb and artificial insemination. In this give and take it is the task of the chaplain to contribute the depth of understanding and perspective derived from a biblical faith. Over the years lay leaders, who have then been trained as group organizers in their own right, have arisen in the shops. The startling fact is that after fifteen years no attempt has yet been made to relate the worker to the churches of Sheffield. Wickham has good evidence that when a worker does wander back to one of the traditional parishes, he is all too likely to be absorbed in the activities of the institution, develop a somewhat pharisaical attitude, and end up being of little use in witnessing to the gospel in his factory role.

Wickham is strong medicine for us, as he clearly showed during his recent visit to America. Winsome and charming, he kept asking if our churches were actually dealing with real issues at all. "How," he would ask, "are you Christians really fighting against the principalities and powers that seek to rule the world in defiance to the Lordship of Jesus Christ?" His phrase, "the secular relevance of the Gospel," strikes a rather harsh note for most of us. In other words we must ask ourselves if we are really getting at the heart of man's need in our current vogue of religious discussion and debate.

In Mainz-Kastel, Germany, another interesting industrial chaplain has worked for many years with a concern similar to Wickham's. His name is Horst Symanowski. He himself works for part of each year in neighboring factories, but his primary attention is directed to a resident center for apprentices and theological students who, for six months at a stretch, are exposed to work in the factory, to life with these young industrial workers, and to seminars in which they seek to understand the relevance of the gospel to the problems of modern industrial society. One interesting sidelight of Symanowski's work is his sermon seminar. He long since discovered the boredom with which workers, when they attend church, sit through the sermon. They universally found the preaching of the church dull and irrelevant. Pastor Symanowski holds a sermon writing seminar in his office each Friday evening. A group of ten or twelve workers gather around his desk to discuss the text and help him prepare his Sunday sermon. In the process of getting the sermon written, he not only has the stimulation of the real challenges and questions which arise in the workers' minds but the workers are recipients of stirring and challenging teaching.

In all these situations the men concerned are seeking to remind us again and again that we have no right to talk to the world on our own terms. If we are to communicate the gospel, we must learn to communicate directly with our fellow men on the level of our common humanity. Once this kind of ordinary communication has been established, we may have the occasion to speak about and witness to the meaning of the gospel. But it must be in the world where this is done, in ways that the world can understand and test. We must give up expecting the world to come into the churches to hear us, if the world is to know about the power of Jesus Christ.

In several places in the United States attempts based upon the experience of the Evangelical Academies or the work of Ted Wickham have been undertaken. Notable among these is the Detroit Industrial Mission of the Episcopal Diocese of Michigan, one of whose leaders worked for several years with Wickham in Sheffield. The experience of the industrial chaplain idea in America, however, has been relatively unsuccessful. Too often the chaplain becomes a function of the personnel department of the factory, giving most of his time to counselling. Our problem seems to be not demonstrating the secular relevance of the gospel to a suspicious or antagonistic world, but rather finding ways of engaging the world in a conversation at levels that really have significance. Not only has the frontier between the church and the world been lost, but as Paul Tillich has several times said, we have lost the dimension of depth in our religious life.

2. CHURCH CENTERED: THE CONGREGATION IN MISSION

The Iona Community, through its ministry in parishes of the Church of Scotland, has gained considerable experience and wisdom in the mission of the church. The books which have emerged from the experience of the community, as well as their little journal, *The Coracle,* are directly relevant to much of our American church life.[1] In their discussion the ministers of the Iona Community have given considerable attention to the life of the congregation in worship, preaching, and also to the mission of the church. A chapter in one of MacLeod's books is

---

[1] See George F. MacLeod, *We Shall Rebuild* (Glasgow: Iona Community Publishing House); George F. MacLeod, *Only One Way Left* (Glasgow: Iona Community Publishing House, 1956); T. R. Morton, *What Is the Iona Community?* (Glasgow: Iona Community Publishing House, 1958); T. R. Morton, *The Twelve Together* (Glasgow: Iona Community Publishing House, 1956).

entitled "The Congregation, an Instrument of Mission." The thesis is simple: the work of a congregation is mission, and its whole life must be directed outward to its witness in the world. In very concrete ways the Iona Community has developed a pattern of congregational mission on an intensive basis that involves different emphases during the course of a period of several years.

While not himself a member of the Iona Community, Tom Allan in *The Face of My Parish* gives a full scale and very moving picture of a parish mission that followed substantially the pattern developed by churches served by Iona Community ministers. This is as good a book on "practical theology" as one can find, for in the best sense it combines theology and practice. In concrete steps it describes the renewal of a largely dormant, downtown, Glasgow church, when slowly and carefully a core of people within its life began to turn their eyes outward to the community around the church and developed a genuine sense of mission.

3. AMERICAN EVANGELISM

Wherever one discusses evangelism in the American scene, two aspects are at once important. On the one hand there has been the great tradition of revivalism exemplified in our time by the crusades of Billy Graham. On the other hand many of our large Protestant denominations have given tremendous emphasis to different types of visitation evangelism, which has been the major thrust of these denominations in terms of their mission in the world. Both have a certain irrelevance about them.

In New York City we recently were subjected to the Billy Graham campaign. In a great metropolis like New York, with the incredible depersonalization described earlier, someone standing up and speaking to a huge crowd of people is nothing more than a peddler of the gospel. Such a campaign may even serve to inoculate great sections of the population against the gospel for many years to come. The evangelistic thrust of the church in urban centers must be through an expression of love in action and through the witness of the fellowship of the Christian community. It is *diakonia* and *koinonia*, not *kerygma*, with which the city of New York must initially be confronted if it is to know the reality of Jesus Christ. As a revivalist Billy Graham calls back those who have been faithful before; he is not an apostle who calls them for the first time to faith in Jesus Christ as Lord. In the face of the fantastic areas of New York City, in which the witness of the gospel is almost entirely absent, it seems a tragedy that major Protestant forces there should unite in one great crusade which, in the end, reveals only a very great ignorance about the basic way in which the witness and mission of the church must be fulfilled in our day.

Objections must also be raised about normal processes of visitation evangelism. They also have a way of betraying the gospel, for in so many of these programs we act like little more than life insurance salesmen. It is easy to parody the procedures which so often develop. In a way it is quite unfair to the denominational executives who devise the literature. But if in fact the men who carry out these campaigns grossly misunderstand the gospel in spite of the materials in their hands, then we must be hesitant about our use of this system. Often people in such campaigns are sent out with the enthusiasm of life insurance salesmen to sell a product. This kind of business terminology is absolutely blasphemous in terms of presenting the claims of Jesus Christ. If our appeal is basically, "Look how much the church has done for me; come and be a part of it for your own sake," then we are giving people a serious distortion of the truth of the gospel. When we sell the church as a good thing for the community and thus something which we must support, we distort the gospel. When we urge people to participate in the life of the church because it will be good for their children, we distort the gospel. When we urge people to join our church because we have an exciting program of activities or a dynamic preacher, we distort the gospel.

Any program of evangelism aimed primarily at getting people into the institutional life of the church is false. Almost inevitably the end of the process is then nothing more than their participation in the life of the congregation, a religious ghetto cut off from the major concerns in the significant arenas of the person's life. The serious claims of Christ upon every area of life go unrecognized. The church too easily becomes another human institution, meeting only the natural needs of men but demanding no renewal of our nature.

There is a very striking phrase which comes from the former Study Secretary for Evangelism in the World Council of Churches, D. T. Niles. Evangelism, he says, is "one beggar telling another beggar where to find food." These are very pregnant words, whose meaning takes on deeper aspects every time I read them. They are clearly spoken against the idea of those who say, "I have become rich; come and share at my table." The Christian is still a beggar who stands in the same predicament of hunger and sinfulness as his fellow men, but he is able to point to the source of food for both their hungers, to Jesus Christ, the Lord of the church.

In spite of my distress over much that goes by the name of visitation evangelism, I am still persuaded that in our experiments in this direction in the United States we have developed some very remarkable means of witnessing to the Lord of the Church. Not a few of the denominations have taken a second look at their earlier scalp-taking raids and have developed a program of training for leaders that has begun to deal with many of the objections to this method.

It seems to me the problem of visitation evangelism is primarily that of not permitting the visitation to take priority over the evangelism. We cannot evangelize anyone until we have established a relationship with him as a fellow human being and have gained the right to converse

124

with him on the level of our ordinary human concerns. This is not an easy thing to do in the depersonalization of our big cities. In our parish a new housing project is erected with 1,400 families in a dozen buildings. Members of the parish are sent around to call on various families. It is a very discouraging business. People in a housing project often wish simply to be left alone; they do not want to put down roots in a community where they feel they are transients, nor do they want to run the risk of getting involved with other people who are strangers. Furthermore, when someone from the church comes around to knock on the door, he is following the pattern of a dozen other salesmen a day. When a knock comes on the door in an East Harlem housing project, one automatically assumes not that it is a friend coming to call but a huckster trying to sell you something. It is almost impossible for the representative of the church not to be put into the category of just another salesman, trying to sell you on coming to his church and buying his product. Again and again, as a result of a first visit, the Christian is greeted with a certain amount of reserve and gotten rid of as quickly as possible with the promise, "Oh, you're from the church across the street? I'll plan to come, maybe this Sunday," and the door is hastily closed. The salesman has been eliminated, at least for the time being, and forgotten.

But that's only the first step. A week later it is important to go back again. When the door is opened and the caller is recognized as that person from the church, there is apt to be an immediate surge of guilt and some excuses for not having attended. Meanwhile, the visitor has walked in and sat down and said something like this, "Well, how are things going?" and in every possible way disowned any interest in talking about his supposed product—the church. This is a rather confusing approach to the person who lives in the apartment, and he doesn't quite get your angle. Why do you seem so interested in just talking about what's going on and not in getting down to business?

This is precisely, however, why you are there. The church must come in friendship and concern to know, on a level of common human concourse, the people who are part of this parish. We are not peddling our product but coming as brothers to know who it is that God has placed in our midst. This has got to be genuine; it cannot be a new tactic for scalp taking, but the caller must genuinely wish to know the person upon whom he is calling.

Is this not clearly implying that we can evangelize no one unless we are servant to him? It is the task of the visitation evangelist not to knock on one thousand doors but to come to know one or two or three families on a basis of friendship and interest, and above all by placing himself at their disposal as a Christian called to be a servant. This is to plow, to sow, to nurture, and hopefully to harvest; it is not to force some kind of growth upon the soil nor to reap before God has given the increase. When visitation evangelism shortcircuits this process and makes it quite apparent that you want to get the persons from where they are to where you are, it is false. When our first job is not to sell them a bill of goods or to get them into our institution but to know them as people with a name and a history, then we are on the right track. We must come because they live here, and we want to know who they are, and we must be willing to stay on this basis although they never darken our church door. Unless we have this willingness, the pretense of wanting to get to know them is hypocrisy.

This is a confusing and baffling thing to the people of this world. Again and again it opens the doors through which they are led into the arena of conversion. When the evangelist knows that his task is simply this and that he rightly may leave the outcome in God's hands, then, having done all he can, he may go to his rest in the trust that God gives whatever growth is destined to come. But while he trusts in God, he also exists in expectancy. We must always be ready for the moment when the right word can be spoken. When we are seeking

office. Even the word "layman" is a rather unfortunate term, for it means someone who is rather ignorant in a particular field. If I say to a doctor, "I am a layman in your field," it means I know nothing about medicine. If one may use a rather unbiblical metaphor, the minister is usually looked upon as the star of the team. He is Mickey Mantle, the star center fielder of the New York Yankees, who hits all the home runs and makes the headlines. This is dead wrong. The minister should be in a role like that of Casey Stengel, the manager of the team. The game, that is the real task of the colony, is outside its walls in the world. The work of the colonists is where they spend their lives. As Casey Stengel must sit on the bench during the game, so the minister is called to work within the life of the colony. He is to prepare the colonists for their work and ministry in the world. He is to preach and teach and edify the body, but he cannot himself be the colonist any more than Casey Stengel can jump off the bench when the Yankees are being defeated and put himself in as a pinch hitter. The ministry, that is to say the ordained clergy, exists in the church for the sake of the world, and the laity exists in the world for the sake of the church.

It is this kind of concern about the role of the laity which is being emphasized by remarkable documents emanating from the Department on the Laity of the World Council of Churches, and in particular in their publication, *The Laity,* and through a whole host of lay conferences and study programs emerging in Europe.

The same kind of emphasis underlies the work of a quite significant development at the University of Texas, called the Christian Faith and Life Community. For a number of years, small groups of students have lived together under a discipline of life and study designed to help them fulfill their Christian obedience in their involvement in the life of the University. Here very useful thinking has been done about the role of the laymen. The parish life conferences of the Episcopal

Church have also been a way of bringing the layman to the recognition of his legitimate role as the colonist.

For the preparation of the Christian to witness in his life in dispersion, the minister is necessary. For the actual work in the world he is by and large irrelevant. Many clergy would dispute this claim, but I have long since become persuaded that when I myself engage in visitation evangelism, I confirm the assumption that the person at the door is a salesman. I am paid to work for the church. But when a layman calls, it is immensely more effective. Further, in the world itself, in the midst of the social structures in which individual lives are bound, it is our laymen who are there now, who have the opportunity of "gossiping about the gospel," of entering casually into a dialogue with the individual nearby in a way that is utterly denied to the minister who inevitably comes as an intruder into a situation about which he knows little. As long as the minister permits himself, in the most subtle ways, to stand at the forefront of the missionary work of the church, he will to that degree inhibit the laity from fulfilling their legitimate function as colonists and thus obstruct the creation of a situation in which the genuine renewal of the church may be given by God.

Laymen, then, must be called upon to fulfill their work as Christians through their witness in the world. This is clearly and unambiguously the work of the church. At the same time there is the work of the church which involves the life of the colony itself. This is really the secondary work of the Christian. This is the troops of supply; this is the work of preparation, rather than the primary task to be engaged in. Most churches have the matter precisely reversed. Church work is what you do in the church building. And work within the church building, as most of us know, is primarily institutional, that is to say, raising money for the church, keeping the institutional activities operating efficiently and the building in repair.

Biblically, in all this we really are in no man's land. The New Testament hardly gives us a clue on the problems which arise in any of these areas. As a matter of fact, when the New Testament speaks about the life of the church itself, it is concerned about rather strikingly different matters. A most significant passage is in Paul's letter to the Ephesians.

And his gifts were that some should be apostles, some prophets, some evangelists, some pastors and teachers, for the equipment of the saints, for the work of ministry, for building up the body of Christ, until we all attain to the unity of the faith and of the knowledge of the Son of God, to mature manhood, to the measure of the stature of the fulness of Christ.

Eph. 4:11-13

Again in the twelfth chapter of First Corinthians, the implications are clear that in the church people are given various gifts of ministry. It seems that each is expected to have a particular gift to be used on behalf of the congregation. Some are teachers; some are preachers, some apostles, some healers, some administrators, etc.

This stands in contrast to the generally prevalent assumption that the minister is supposed to be *par excellence* gifted in each of these ways. Listen to most charges at ordinations, and you will discover that the minister is expected to be a great teacher, preacher, priest, pastor, apostle, and all the rest. He is supposed to have, to a remarkable degree, been gifted in these many different directions. The implications of this passage in Ephesians makes clear the senselessness of this position. We can hardly expect that God would wrap up in one person all these gifts, many of which may be actually contradictory. Does it follow that a man whom God has called as a gifted preacher will be particularly useful as an administrator? Those with great gifts in healing may be of no use whatsoever in teaching. Of course, the result is that the layman, with his own little gift, whatever it is, is simply a kind of as-

131

sistant to the minister, who has the prior and useful gift in any particular area of the congregation's life.

The problem comes from both ends. As long as congregations hire
ministers to do all these different tasks and expect them to be gifted in
these incredibly different ways, we will defeat the ministry of the
laity. As long as we clergy continue to need the psychological sense of
being top dog in the whole church and insist on exerting our authority
in every possible area, we will defeat the ministry of the laity.

The task of the ordained clergyman, specifically in the tradition of
the Reformation, to which I am committed, is first of all to preach the
true and lively word of God, with power and faithfulness as God gives
it to him; secondly, to lead the sacramental life of the congregation;
and third, to release, train, and direct the gifts of the Holy Spirit,
which by God's grace have been poured into the common life of the
congregation. Again he is the coach or the trainer whose job it is to
see that the very gifts of ministry are fully utilized for the sake of the
common good. Again and again this means for ministers restricting
their work to what may at first be rather confining areas. It means a
tremendous battle against the present expectations of what our task
is as now defined by the American churches. But again it is the integrity of the gospel which is at stake. When I spend 80 per cent of
my week doing tasks other than preaching or preparing to preach the
gospel, administering or preparing to administer the sacraments, edi-
fying or training or preparing to edify and train the saints of the
church, then I am not being a clergyman and am doing my work as
a layman and in actual fact cheating the congregation of the full-time
services of an ordained minister.

As we all know, volumes of literature are being written about the
task of the minister in our day, but we are often on the horns of a
very false dilemma. If we simply try to figure out how to become better
administrators or more able to deal with the multiplicity of tasks which

are thrown our way, we are defeated. Instead, we must wage a major battle against the variety of functions which, it is assumed, must be performed by us in the first place. I am well aware that this will be a difficult task, and we will make headway only if we begin again to subject our lives as Christians to the judgment of the New Testament and of our own heritage. At the same time the problem may well be solved only if the clergy itself is willing to recognize its own ego involvement in the problem.

The real miracle that took place through the apostleship of Paul points in this same direction. Based on the experience of modern missions, it is really fantastic to realize that Paul went into a pagan community, preached the gospel in the synagog until he was put out, and then on the street corner. Yet within a matter of months, he gathered together, by the power of the Holy Spirit, a small congregation of Christians. Within a matter of a very few months Paul had discovered that in the congregation gifts of the Holy Spirit were given the saints. He offered them some brief training and direction and then went his way, leaving them to struggle. At whatever cost this method involved, at least these young Christians were not dependent upon the continual presence of the missionary in their midst but forced to grow up to mature manhood, looking for their life to the power of the Holy Spirit and not to their founder.[1] We clergy must dare trust the Holy Spirit to utilize the members of our congregation for the tasks which we hold so closely pressed to ourselves. Even so, the congregations must be willing to expose themselves to the empowerment and gifting of the Holy Spirit and willing within the life of the household of faith to exercise these gifts.

One other point about this passage from Eph. 4, was first called to my attention by Hans-Reudi Weber, Secretary of the Department of Laity of the World Council of Churches. He noted that in the Revised

---

[1] See the remarkable book by Roland Allen, *Missionary Methods, St. Paul's or Ours?*

Standard Version the translation is not quite correct, but rather should be altered to read in verses eleven and twelve, "and his gifts were that some should be apostles, some prophets, some evangelists, some pastors and teachers *in order to* equip the saints for the work of ministry." These gifts, given to the congregation, again turn us in the direction of our mission. Our life within the congregation and the use of these gifts are *in order to* prepare the whole body of the church for its ministry, its mission which is lived apart from the life of the colony. The ministry of all believers, exercising the gifts of the Holy Spirit, would place in proper perspective the particular ministry of the ordained clergy.

To recapitulate, the work of the ordained clergy is within the life of the church for the sake of the world, while the work of the laity is primarily in the world for the sake of the church. The minister is not the colonist. He is the trainer of the colonists; he does not represent the church in the world but within the congregation is called upon to proclaim God's word and enable God's people to see again and again more clearly the task to which they are called through their common life together. This is a particular task within the church which the minister must exercise with faithfulness and care. He, in a sense, lives on the other frontier, the one that is between God and man. It is this boundary which he must know well. Before God he is every man, facing the same doubts, loneliness, and fears that beset everyone in our world today. When he preaches, he is preaching to himself as much as to the congregation. No minister dare separate himself from the common life of men, even by virtue of his sacred calling. But at the same moment, within the congregation, the minister must be the spokesman for God. He is called upon to preach God's living word to the congregation, to make God's word in the Sacrament manifest. He is a pilot called upon not to entertain the passengers but to steer the ship.

When the laity of a local church come to understand their task in relation to that of the ordained clergy, then they become colonists, not as second rate assistants to the professionals but as those rightly called by God to serve as his witnesses in the world. The laymen are the servants who, in every relation with their neighbors, seek to embody the spirit of the Good Samaritan and thus reflect the love of Christ. They enter into organizations that work for justice as part of their service to their Lord. Politics becomes an arena in which their obedience is rightfully expressed. The colonist also sees with eyes of faith the ultimate need of his brother and with patience and much prayer awaits the moment when he may speak of the Lord of Life, who sustains him in his ministry. His own life, in all that he does, is an offering to God.

CHAPTER VIII

THE INTEGRITY OF THE CHURCH

So put away all malice and all guile and insincerity and envy and all slander. Like newborn babes, long for the pure spiritual milk, that by it you may grow up to salvation; for you have tasted the kindness of the Lord. Come to him, to that living stone, rejected by men but in God's sight chosen and precious; and like living stones be yourselves built into a spiritual house, to be a holy priesthood, to offer spiritual sacrifices acceptable to God through Jesus Christ. . . . But you are a chosen race, a royal priesthood, a holy nation, God's own people, that you may declare the wonderful deeds of him who called you out of darkness into his marvelous light. Once you were no people but now you are God's people; once you had not received mercy but now you have received mercy.

I Pet. 2:1-5, 9-10

How can we who call ourselves Christians accept the implications of this title and place upon ourselves the mark of Jesus Christ and not take seriously the implications of this in the concrete situation where our lives have been placed? There is a necessary correspondence between what we affirm and what we do as God's people. When this is lacking, the church is seriously weakened or destroyed. Do we really know that God has called us from darkness into light, that once we were no people, but now we are God's people? Then the substance of our life is worship, for we rejoice in what God has done. The purpose of our life is God's purpose, "that you may declare the wonderful deeds of him who called you out of darkness into his marvelous light." We come apart from the world into the colony for worship and renewal out of a sense of gratitude and need, for in the world the battle is fierce. We are sent back from the colony into the world because this is the task to which God has called us. There are clear patterns of life, both for the individual and for the congregation or the colony, structures through which it may be possible for the integrity of the church to exist, though these structures can never create it. They are wineskins to contain the gospel.

As these chapters have been urging, the integrity of the church depends upon our understanding of the missionary nature of the church. When a church seeks in its whole life to prepare its members for mission, then it is fulfilling its proper function under the providence of God. It has integrity, that is, a correspondence between what it affirms and what it is and does. Or put more correctly, there is a correspondence between what God has done and what we are doing. In the deepest sense the Church has its own integrity in Jesus Christ. But we can easily confess him with our lips and ignore the implications. The church exists for the world. It exists to witness by its service to love where there is hate. It witnesses to *koinonia* where there is depersonalization and brokenness. It witnesses to the power and Lordship of Christ where the principalities and powers of evil warp and twist and destroy human life. But this is all pious talk unless this is entered into with total seriousness.

The integrity of our life as Christians depends upon establishing patterns of a disciplined life, both together and in our individual situations, that will so sustain us and nurture our lives that by God's mercy we "may grow up to salvation." One suspects that 99 and 44/100 per cent of the church members of our country are indeed newborn babes who need the gentlest possible diet as they begin to toddle and walk. As for a child a key word must be discipline. There are certain habit patterns which must be instilled in us if our obedience to Christ is to have expression. A new birth really implies that even our natural instincts may be subject to change. Integrity made possible by discipline is not a way of improving my own character or making myself more pious but entirely and solely in order that God may better be able to use the instrument of my life as a witness for himself.

In quite specific terms I would suggest several areas in which the problem of integrity looms large, and where it may be that the dimensions of the new wineskins are emerging. Each is marked with dangers of Pharisaism or superficiality or sentimentality, but these are risks which we must take in the face of the predicament of the church.

A. The Habits of the Christian Life

As Christians we are both part of a worshiping fellowship and at the same time must live part of our life alone. Earlier we have discussed at length something of the "style of life" that seems crucial for the churches of our day. The integrity of the church is deeply related to our faithfulness in finding the new wineskins through which our corporate life can find expression. But integrity also depends in no small way upon the willingness of Christians individually to struggle with the appropriate habit patterns for their lives. In his unusual book, *Life Together,* Dietrich Bonhoeffer speaks of the fact that the true believer must find a pattern for his life in the times when he is alone as well as a pattern for his life when he is together with other Christians. Intimate and necessary as our relation is with our fellow Christians, each man stands uniquely alone before God.

The Iona Community in Scotland and the Kirkridge movement in this country, patterned somewhat after the experience of Iona, have both stressed the deep need for clergy and laity alike to develop patterns of discipline in their Christian life which enable them to take seriously the claim of Christ. Those groups have much to say about the experience which they have accumulated over the years, not least of all the witness to the tremendous difficulty of bringing Protestant ministers to accept any kind of discipline, even though they themselves impose it. Too much are we creatures of habit who, even when we offer our lives to Christ, resent in all kinds of subtle and occasionally unconscious ways the necessity of changing our basic patterns of life and thought. In our need we accept Christ, but as time passes, more and more we set the terms of the relationship. The East Harlem Protestant Parish, at the beginning, also sensed the same need for the clergy to define some patterns of discipline that would mutually sustain us. Increasingly, we have discovered that the clergy at some peril devised a special discipline for themselves, which seems to infer that they are striving for a higher quality of Christian life than the ordinary layman's. Increasingly, the disciplines of the Parish have been those that have been urged, as necessary for all Christians, to be applied at only a few points with special reference to the individual Christian's own calling within the life of the church. The present pattern is in general along these lines.[1]

1. THE ORDERED DAY

If we are, with seriousness, to offer each day to God, presenting to him its work and play, the total life of our day, then it is necessary that we give thought to how we shall meet the demands which will come to us. The day should begin with thankfulness for the night's rest and meditation in which we seek to plan how we will make use of this day that God has given us. This ordering of the day includes intercession for those whose lives will touch ours this day, petitions for ourselves and our needs, thanksgiving and confession. This is customarily also a time when the daily lectionary is read and time taken

---

[1] For further information about this pattern and the work of the East Harlem Protestant Parish in general write to 2050 Second Ave. New York 29, N.Y.

for Bible study. It is not surprising that when one has given thought to one's day, there is a sacramental quality given to it that otherwise is lacking. It is also not surprising that God frequently interrupts our day and we must be prepared to give up plans which we made, but not carelessly or accidentally. All too easily clergymen, even more readily than laymen, permit the events of the day and the demands placed upon them by the world to determine almost totally how they will spend their time, rather than seeking to follow a pattern which they have determined in God's sight to be right. An ordered day also means that when our time of rest draws near, we look back upon the events of the day with thanksgiving for the joys and meaning which have come, with confession in very specific ways for those things which we have done which we should not have done, and for the opportunities which we have missed, confessing the very concrete and specific sinfulness of our day. We intercede for those whose lives have touched ours and who stand in need of God's love and care, offering up our own petitions. Having done our day's work, we commit our lives into God's hands and go to sleep.

2. WEEKLY ATTENDANCE AT HOLY COMMUNION AND FAITHFUL PARTICIPA-
TION IN THE WORSHIP LIFE OF A CONGREGATION

At the moment in the East Harlem Protestant Parish the clergy commit themselves to a weekly service of Holy Communion, in addition to the regular eleven o'clock service, while the laity are expected only to attend Communion service in the regular eleven o'clock worship on the first Sunday of each month. As indicated earlier the stress in the service of worship is upon the preaching of the Word and on the whole drama of salvation enacted in the Sacrament of Holy Communion.

3. TO PARTICIPATE WEEKLY IN AN "ENABLING GROUP" WITH FELLOW
CHRISTIANS

At the present time the major emphasis is upon Bible study, both for clergy and laity although other groups, such as a Brotherhood of Christian Workers, are also meeting. These cell groups or prayer fellowships or whatever we call them must again and again be checked to discover the degree in which they are in fact the arena in which the real problems of our life as Christians in the world are being considered. Too easily we find ways of avoiding, through our pious exercises, real confrontation with God's demand for obedience in our life in the world.

4. WE PLEDGE OURSELVES ONCE A MONTH TO DISCUSS OUR CHRISTIAN FAITH AND THE CONCRETE FULFILLMENT OF OUR CALLING WITHIN OUR LIFE IN CHRIST WITH ONE BROTHER WHOM WE SELECT

It has been interesting to discover that there are certain ways in which God speaks to us through our relationship to a study group of those whom we come to know well. There is quite another set of relationships established when we must discuss, in very concrete ways, our adherence to the discipline which we have accepted and consider with a brother the precise ways in which we are fulfilling our vocation as clergy or whatever. There is a kind of inescapable honesty to which one is driven in the individual relationship. When one must confess, as so frequently is the case, his own failure to adhere to aspects of the discipline to which he is pledged or is called upon in love to examine the inadequate way in which he is fulfilling his obligation to God, it is a very humbling and very powerful business. I hesitate to refer to this relationship which we have discovered as a very vital and necessary one in terms of Bonhoeffer's "confessor," for this is a little too strong a word for Protestants. Yet in effect that is precisely the direction in which we seem to be moving. A Christian has real need for a brother in Christ, who for him acts as a confessor and spiritual guide. Perhaps the very painfulness of this kind of relationship and the way in which we, in our situation in East Harlem, have managed to avoid it at every opportunity indicates how really necessary this kind of relationship is for our life in Christ.

5. TO GIVE REGULARLY A DEFINITE SHARE OF ONE'S INCOME TO GOD'S CHURCH

In recognition of our dependence upon God, we render unto him, in joyful thanksgiving, a part of what he has given us.

6. TO PARTICIPATE IN AT LEAST ONE COMMUNITY ORGANIZATION WORKING FOR JUSTICE OR BROTHERHOOD

This is a symbol of our responsibility to witness in concrete ways to the love of God in Christ. For members of our parish we are trying to say, "Your service to the church, your work as Christians is symbolized by your participation in at least one community organization such as the NAACP, The American Civil Liberties Union, the Urban League, the local political party, or the PTA." This is a reminder that all of our work and life in the world serves to witness to Jesus Christ or perhaps against him.

7. TO EXERCISE FAITHFULLY THE PARTICULAR MINISTRY WHICH HAS BEEN GIVEN US IN THE FELLOWSHIP OF THE CHURCH

In the light of Eph. 4:11-12, each Christian must seek to find the particular gift which he can exercise on behalf of the congregation in order that all may be more adequately prepared for their ministry in the world.

We might summarize like this: Most of us are half-time or half-baked Christians. In certain areas of life or at certain times and in certain relationships we seek to fulfill our obedience to Jesus Christ and live by his claims. By and large, however, our faith is not the central focus through which we look at the world. We affirm the Lordship of Christ over only part of what we do or part of what we are. But this is ridiculous. Either he is Lord of life, or he is not. To take seriously his Lordship over our lives means to take with utter seriousness these patterns of discipline. They enable us to develop, as children in Christ, the habits appropriate to our new life. Perhaps the several I have outlined here must be radically modified or are not appropriate for all. I am persuaded, however, that patterns of discipline are absolutely necessary if the integrity of the church is to be maintained. These disciplines are not legalism; they are for here and now in the particular form in which we express them, but they must take into account the fulness of our life in Christ and are clearly necessary for the pastoral integrity of the church. If Jesus is the Lord of life, we must expose our whole life to him.

B. The Need to Mark the Boundaries

Whether it be in East Harlem, where it is faced with a hostile and antagonistic world, or in suburbia, where the gospel too easily is accepted, the colony must still protect the integrity of its existence by the seriousness with which it takes the right to participate in its inner life. If, when we withdraw from our task in the world into the protection and renewing power of the colony, we bring the world with us, we may well be destroyed. I am under the impression that many American churches of our time day by day are bringing the Trojan horse into the midst of their common life and quickly falling prey to the infiltrations of the enemy without even being aware of the disaster which has overtaken them. It is of necessity that we draw apart behind the walls of the colony, not because we hate the world or are seeking to rid ourselves of it, but precisely in order to have the strength, wisdom, and courage to return to our calling in the midst of the world. It is a sobering concern if in fact the world walks in the door with us every time we come apart into the church, and thus the life of the congregation is confused and diluted.

There are several points at which this frontier between the world and the church must be clearly defined and carefully defended against the assaults of the enemy. The first is church membership. The witness of the Church of the Saviour in Washington, D.C., sounds at least strenuous and often preposterous to most of us. To become a member of this remarkable congregation requires a minimum time of at least two years following your initial decision to commit yourself to the church. During this time you are expected to be a regular participant in the life of the congregation, but you must use this period in order to study and prepare yourself that you may know with soberness that you are willing to commit your life to Jesus Christ. The congregation is quite clear in pointing out that they do not wish to exclude anyone, but at the same time they feel it is not fair to permit a person to stand up before the congregation and pledge himself to participate in its life and to acknowledge Jesus Christ as Lord without really knowing what this means by having some opportunity to explore the implications of obedience before taking this concrete step. They do not wish the church to be like the woman who marries an alcoholic to reform him. It does not work as well as to demand before marriage some evidence that the alcoholic's desire for reformation is indeed serious.

In talking with the minister of this congregation, one is impressed by his understanding of the problems of such an approach and by his deep feeling that here is a vital witness to be made. One is even more impressed by meeting the congregation and discovering here the tremendous vitality and sense of power that bespeaks God's presence in the midst of these people. Significantly, the last time I talked with Gordon Cosby, pastor of the church, I asked about the size of their congregation. He replied that it had now grown too large for their liking. With some seventy committed members it was somewhat unwieldy for the kind of intimate fellowship he believed the body of Christ must have.

In the midst of the conversation with Cosby, the pastor of a large suburban church, where we were waiting for an ordination to begin, came up to us. Jokingly, I asked him, "What are your problems?" His response was, "Oh, we've got a really serious issue. We have no place for people to park on Sunday morning. If we just had better parking facilities, our membership could jump a thousand in six months."

Here, as sharply put as one could find it, is the contrasting approach of two churches on the matter of church membership. The important thing to note is that the Church of the Saviour of Washington, D.C., is not radically sectarian in the sense that it wishes to separate itself in moral purity from the world. Rather, it stands in the Reformation tradition and seeks to take seriously the matter of membership only in order that its call to witness may better be fulfilled. It may be blasphemous to make judgments, but I strongly suspect that Church of the Saviour, with its seventy-seven members, was at that moment making a far more significant witness in Washington, D.C., to the Lordship of Jesus Christ than the church which then had two thousand members and which, within six months by the simple expedient of spending eighty thousand dollars to purchase and demolish four houses on the corner across the street and thus secure a parking lot, would have a thousand additional members.

There are two New Testament passages which must be taken seriously; neither one is comfortable. In the second chapter of the Book of Acts Peter preaches the magnificent Pentecost sermon. At its conclusion, according to Acts 2:37-38, the results were as follows:

Now when they heard this they were cut to the heart, and said to Peter and the rest of the apostles, "Brethren what shall we do?" And Peter said to them, "Repent, and be baptized every one of you in the name of Jesus Christ for the forgiveness of your sins; and you shall receive the gift of the Holy Spirit."

Is there something here that we must also use in considering the requirements for joining one of our churches? The elements included

145

here are significant. First of all they were "cut to the heart." They indentified themselves with those who had crucified Christ and really felt the anguish of their own sin. In the face of Jesus Christ they saw themselves as sinful men, and the response was an anguished cry. They were cut to the heart; they wanted to know what they could do. Peter's reply was simple, "Repent and be baptized for the forgiveness of your sins." Is this by any chance a necessary indication of conversion? Do we have the right to expect those who commit their lives to Jesus Christ to know themselves as sinners, genuinely to have repented, and to have some sense of the power of forgiveness in their lives? At some point we must have seen ourselves clearly in the mirror of Christ and shuddered. It may well be that the experience that has led us to a genuine overturning of life may have been at a different point than recognizing Jesus Christ as Lord. In the face of our lonely or broken life the discovery of the Christian fellowship may have had a similarly transforming experience.

Another passage in the New Testament suggests the way in which our confrontation with the gospel may come through the problem of our obedience in the world. I refer to the story of the rich young ruler who asked Jesus what he might do to be saved. According to the New Testament description, Jesus looked at him with compassion and asked if he had fulfilled the commands of God. The young man replied that he had kept the law and done all that was required. Here indeed was a person with a superb ethical life who had given himself to full obedience but was still concerned that something was lacking and had thus been led to this conversation. Looking into the heart of the man, Jesus recognized that his obedience was not enough. He had to make it clear to the young man that if he wished truly to find the meaning of his life, he must be willing to give up whatever human possessions he held most dear and commit his life to a new Lord. He must take orders from another source. For this particular individual the most important thing in his life was his money. Therefore, the response was obvious; he must sell all that he had and get rid of the funds, as a symbol that money no longer was the idol of his life. The response was a sad one, for the young man knew himself well enough that, faced with this demand, he turned and sadly walked away. It is sad when we must speak a word that turns a sinner away from God's household.

Whenever I use this illustration in a talk, I almost inevitably get into a severe argument and am heartily challenged. What Protestant church that any of us knows would have let a young man like this get away? In most churches, with his fine character and good presence, he would have been an officer in six months. He's exactly the kind of person we want in our churches—bright, attractive, upstanding, honorable young citizen. But Jesus didn't accept him, and that's the point. Note especially that the rejection was not a legalistic one, nor did Jesus himself pass any judgment upon the man any more than we who are within the colony have the right to pass judgment upon those who submit themselves to us. The point is a somewhat different one. The integrity of the church demands not that we stand in judgment over the lives of others but rather that we make so clear the implications of life in the colony that the individual makes his own judgment. We must say so clearly what it means to accept Jesus Christ as Lord and to participate in the life of the colony that no one takes the decision to commit his life to the church casually or hastily. It means that we must dare to see countless men and women turn away sorrowfully. This is a daring thing for the church to hazard, but it is precisely the witness being made by the Church of the Saviour in Washington, D.C. This is no Pharisaical judgment; it simply says, "these are the conditions." Anyone can meet them, but at the same time they must be taken with total seriousness. Remember also that when the rich young ruler turned away, I suspect that Jesus prayed for him, and we do not know but that by God's grace he may eventually have become a follower. So it is in our situation. We are not excluding men by this method from our prayers or ultimately from their being led into the fellowship of the church.

Another area in which the boundary of the colony must be protected comes in the performance of the sacraments and orders of the church. There is the question of baptism. My own denomination practices infant baptism. I am deeply troubled by the irresponsible way in which I have, in the past, been involved in services of baptism that had little more significance than a pagan ritual and were performed only because of the folklore of a particular situation which says that babies must be baptized. It was something that you did to the child, but it had long since lost any real meaning or significance. Baptism is a mighty act by which a baby or a child is brought into the providence of God's grace, for whom the congregation makes certain promises, and whom we acknowledge to be now under the care of Almighty God and stamped with his mark. Whatever our own theology of baptism it is a significant event in the life of a human being.

Occasionally, a young couple comes, wanting to have their baby baptized, but are not interested in having it done in the church, for that would be a little conspicuous or embarrassing. Neither of them is a church member perhaps, or so nominally related to the church that you don't happen to have seen either before. It turns out that the grandparents are insisting on the baby being baptized, and so they are willing to subject themselves to the brief ordeal. Integrity is at stake. This may be a grand evangelistic opportunity, but I strongly suspect that we have no right to permit this young couple to stand up before the congregation and make pledges on behalf of this child to bring it up in the knowledge and love of God when God couldn't mean less in their lives. Here again there are tremendous dangers of unloving legalism. Yet this is an arena of importance for the integrity of the church. We who are clergy must wrestle with our congregations in order that the meaning of baptism be re-established, and that it become an act performed responsibly within the life of the congregation. I should imagine that this problem of guarding the integrity of baptism is equally pressing in communions which observe believers' baptism.

The problem of marriage is even more difficult. A lovely young couple comes to you to be married. They want a church wedding for all kinds of secular and aesthetic reasons. They will be expected, in the course of the service, to make solemn promises before God. I, the clergyman, marry them only by the right given me by the state, on the assumption that it is a sober act of the church. I would suggest that in spite of the evangelistic implications a clergyman, at very great peril, permits a young couple to be married in the church unless both of them are baptized Christians who have taken the time with him to understand the implications of the vows which they are making and who soberly and honestly are willing to commit their lives to God. Here again the minister has no right to be the final judge but only to define the meaning of Christian marriage in such a way that its implications are absolutely clear. Then if the couple wishes to continue and have him perform the marriage, whether they be honest or not, is a question before God and not for him to judge.

Furthermore, in all of these matters of marking the boundary, the minister dare not stand alone against the congregation. It must be the congregation with the minister who recognizes the need for marking the frontier, so that he is supported by them in his function as the one called to administer the Sacraments of the church. These are important issues with which a congregation ought to be wrestling. Certainly no minister will be able to get away with refusing to marry a couple unless the responsible members of his congregation understand the reasons and support him fully.

149

C. Trusting in the Gospel

In all of this it is not that we are called by God to perfection, or that we will somehow escape the predicament of our sinfulness by efforts of our own will. Anything but this, for God in his own power is able to use us who are still sinful for his own purposes. So great a man as Francis of Assisi was persuaded that the greatest miracle of all was that God was able to use someone as sinful as he, Francis, for God's own work. The Christian is always aware of his own failures before God but always offering his life anew that God might use it. God knows that we shall fail; he will not put before us tasks too great for our strength, but we must know what is central. If in the midst of failure we trust in the gospel, then God can use us in his task of witness. In the church both saint and sinner live by grace. There is no room for self-righteousness.

God chose what is low and despised in the world, even things that are not, to bring to nothing things that are, so that no human being might boast in the presence of God. He is the source of your life in Christ Jesus, whom God made our wisdom, our righteousness and sanctification and redemption.

I Cor. 1:28-30

This is to affirm once again that God asks of us that we be engaged in the battle against the principalities and powers of evil, that we give ourselves as his witnesses fully and completely. Then whether we succeed or whether we fail is in his hands. But this is still a persistent issue in American church life. What are the criteria by which a ministry is to be judged? Frequently in East Harlem we are asked what success we have had and find ourselves at a loss for a satisfactory answer. We are constantly referred to in Protestant publications as one place where the churches are meeting with power the challenge of the inner city.

On the other hand we are faced with pointed questions and criticism from many quarters, including the seven supporting denominations, the seminary field work students (no more critical group exists), and our wives. Many crucial issues arise from the ambiguity of our situation. We are an experiment, but we are also a church. We are an interdenominational mission project, seeking to find our own unity and yet remain faithful to our own denominational heritage. We are big and expensive and thus dependent upon generous mission giving. And above all we are committed to responsibility to the indigenous leadership of the parish churches. All of those matters are, in their own way, important issues.

One sympathetic critic of the parish is afraid that we have forged a theology of failure in the light of the results to date in the ministry of the parish. Yet we affirm this: that God does not require of us success or failure but asks only for our full obedience. We are human, and we do seek signs that our work is fruitful. But we know that we cannot depend for our strength and purpose upon our success in changing the world or overcoming evil or gaining new church members. Our only hope is to live in the world by God's grace and thus to expose to the world the real meaning of evil. In the world of East Harlem we are witnessing to something that we know God has done. It is in the degree to which we reflect this, and not in the extent to which social improvements are made, that we are faithful to our commission.

So must it be for the churches of our day. We dare not trust in signs that indicate the approval of the world. We must trust in the gospel alone, in the hope that lies in the victory of Jesus Christ. To the world this knowledge remains foolishness. Our trust seems nonsense. But in season and out the calling of the church is clear:

To preach to the Gentile the unsearchable riches of Christ, and to make all men see what is the plan of the mystery hidden for ages in God who created all things; that through the church the manifold wisdom of God might now be made known to the principalities and powers in the heavenly place.

Eph. 3:8-10

In confidence that God will use them for his own good purposes, Christians must seek to open their lives to the Holy Spirit, to search for new wineskins by which the gospel may be made known to our world, and to live by God's grace alone.

Sources of Understanding

The following bibliography includes books that have been of particular help to the ministers of the East Harlem Protestant Parish as they have sought to understand the nature of the ministry and the calling of the church.

Allan, Tom. *The Face of My Parish*. New York: Harper & Brothers, 1953. An unusual wedding of theology and practice in an excellent book in "practical theology." This is the story of renewal in a Scottish urban parish, as a nucleus in the congregation came to see the meaning of the church as mission.

Allen, Roland. *Missionary Methods: St. Paul's or Ours?* London: World Dominion Press, 1956. First published in 1912, this book is a remarkable critique of the failure of the missionary venture to take adequate account of the methods of Paul. The author suggests strongly that the patterns of the New Testament ought to be normative for the life of the church in a missionary situation.

Appleton, George. *In His Name*. New York: St. Martin's Press, Inc., 1956. A splendid book of prayers for the church and the world, based on biblical insights. The emphasis is upon the discipline of missionary intercession.

Barth, Markus. *The Broken Wall*. Philadelphia: Judson Press, 1959. An excellent study on the meaning of evangelism in the light of Paul's Letter to the Ephesians. Here biblical scholarship proves its powerful and direct relevance to the task of the church in our day.

Bonhoeffer, Dietrich. *Life Together*. New York: Harper & Brothers, 1954. A powerful and moving study of the Christian life in terms of the necessity of discipline in relation to one's brothers. Helpful also in understanding the patterns of life in solitude.

de Dietrich, Suzanne. *The Witnessing Community*. Philadelphia: The Westminster Press, 1958. The author, long associated with the Ecumenical Institute at Bossey, here defines what it means in our day to belong to God's people. Her method is historical, tracing with insight the record of God's purpose to make the church the witnessing community.

Ellul, Jacques. *The Presence of the Kingdom*. Philadelphia: The Westminster Press, 1951. This is a powerful survey of the situation of the Christian in our modern world. Cutting through the superficial patterns of so much in our church life, he points to the need for a Christian "style of life" that will make the church "present in the world with the effectiveness of the Holy Spirit."

Forsyth, P. T. *The Church and the Sacraments.* London: Independent Press, Ltd., 1917. An excellent free church statement on the centrality and meaning of the sacraments. As in his other writings Forsyth speaks with particular relevance to American churches.

Jenkins, Daniel. *The Protestant Ministry.* Garden City, N. Y.: Doubleday and Co., 1958. A fine study of the role of the ministry in the life of the church. The author writes with unusual profundity and freshness about the predicament of the minister, caught between the demands of the gospel and the expectations of his parishioners.

Kraemer, Hendrik. *A Theology of the Laity.* Philadelphia: Westminster Press, 1959. The first good Protestant treatment of the role of the laity in the life of the church. The laity is seen as an integral part of the church's ministry. The witness of the gospel in our day depends upon utilizing the frozen potential of the laymen, who are in fact already the church, present in the world.

MacLeod, George. *Only One Way Left.* Glasgow: The Iona Community Publishing House, 1956. The leader of the Iona Community here analyzes the predicament of the church. He is a voice of authentic prophecy, calling us back to a fresh vision of God's design right now.

Michonneau, Abbé. *Revolution in a City Parish.* Westminster: Newman Press, 1949. This story of a Roman Catholic parish, in a working class section of Paris, has great relevance for Protestants in the urban setting. Central to the author is the integrity of the church. He insists that we know what activities in the life of a parish are appropriate and what are denials of the gospel. He has been a leader in the liturgical revival.

Morton, T. Ralph. *The Twelve Together.* Glasgow: The Iona Community Publishing House, 1956. The deputy leader of the Iona Community here outlines the essential nature of our life together in Christ. He gives attention to the training of the disciples by Jesus in order to understand the meaning of *koinonia* for us.

Myers, C. Kilmer. *Light the Dark Streets.* Greenwich, Conn.: The Seabury Press, Inc., 1957. This is the story of an Episcopal priest in New York's lower East Side and his love for his parish. The book centers around the problems of gang youngsters and the efforts of God's church to meet their need. A sensitive, moving book.

Newbigin, Lesslie. *The Household of God.* New York: Friendship Press, 1954. The author, long a missionary in South India, discusses the nature of the church itself. He argues that the church is only to be understood in a perspective which is at once eschatological and missionary.

Niles, D. T. *That They May Have Life.* New York: Harper & Brothers, 1951. This is a superb book on evangelism as the mission of the church. We are called, the author affirms, to a continuous witness to the living God, revealed in Christ—"in heroic service and humble kindness" before which the peoples of the world will pause, believe, and reform their lives.

Southcott, Ernest. *The Parish Comes Alive.* New York: Morehouse-Gorham Co., 1956. Canon Southcott has pioneered in the "house-church" pattern. He sees the need to relate the life of the church to the common life of men and this in terms of the corporate expression of the Church's worship and action. This book is the story of the life of a Parish in which new wineskins have been found.

Tillich, Paul. *The Protestant Era.* Chicago: University of Chicago Press, 1948. Tillich states here his formulation of the "Protestant Principle," by which all the patterns which men seek to express their obedience must be constantly brought under judgment. An excellent analysis also of the role of religion in the crisis of today.

Visser 't Hooft, William A. *The Renewal of the Church.* Philadelphia: The Westminster Press, 1956. The author assumes that the need for renewal is an established fact. The relevant questions have to do with the nature of the renewal we seek. Renewal, finally, is a gift of the Holy Spirit but not without preparation that God expects of men.

NOTE: Most of the above authors have written other volumes also of great value, particularly:

Allen, Roland. *The Spontaneous Expansion of the Church.* London: World Dominion Press, 1956.

Bonhoeffer, Dietrich. *The Cost of Discipleship.* New York: The Macmillan Co., 1948.

Kraemer, Hendrik. *The Communication of the Christian Faith.* Philadelphia: The Westminster Press, 1956.

MacLeod, George. *We Shall Rebuild.* Philadelphia: The Westminster Press, 1945.

Morton, T. Ralph. *The Iona Community Story.* Glasgow: The Iona Community Publishing House.

Visser 't Hooft, William A. *The Pressure of Our Common Calling.* New York: Doubleday & Company, Inc., 1959.